JURISDICTION AND ENFORCEMENT OF JUDGMENTS IN CIVIL AND COMMERCIAL MATTERS ECJ JUDGMENTS

SUPPPLEMENT

Edited by
Paolo Galizzi

BIICL
British Institute of
International and
Comparative Law

Published and Distributed by
The British Institute of International and Comparative Law
Charles Clore House, 17 Russell Square, London WC1B 5JP

British Library Cataloguing in Publication Data
A Catalogue record of this book is available from the British Library

ISBN 0–903067–85–4

Printed in Great Britain by Biddles Ltd
Guildford and King's Lynn

Introduction

This supplement to "Jurisdiction and Enforcement of Judgments in Civil and Commercial Matters – ECJ Judgments" includes the full text of the decisions delivered by the European Court of Justice on the 1968 Brussels Convention in 2001 and 2002. Extracts from some of these decisions have already been reproduced in the two main volumes on the case-law of the ECJ on the Brussels Convention. However, it was thought that it would be useful to include the full text of these decisions in this separate supplement to provide quick access to the most current decisions on the Convention.

This supplement contains 8 decisions delivered in 2001 and 2002.

In 2001, the Court delivered only one Order on the Brussels Convention, in the case of *Gaillard v Chekili.* The case dealt with a dispute on Article 16(1) of the Convention, concerning exclusive jurisdiction in proceedings which have as their object rights *in rem* in immovable property.

In 2002, the Court delivered nine decisions on the Convention.

In two instances, the case of *Marseille Fret v Seatrano* and the case of *Reichling v Wampach* the Court issued two Orders dismissing the cases for lack of jurisdiction and therefore such Orders have not been reproduced.

The remaining seven judgments dealt with several provisions of the Convention. On 19 February 2002, the Court delivered its judgment in the *Besix* case, on the interpretation of Articles 5(1) and 2 of the Convention, respectively on jurisdiction in matters relating to contracts and on the general criterion for jurisdiction under the Convention.

In its decision delivered on 27 February 2002, in the *Weber* case, the Court examined again Article 5(1) and in particular the concept of place of performance of a contractual obligation in a contract of employment.

On 6 June 2002, in *Italian Leather*, the Court interpreted Article 27(2) of the Convention and dealt with the problem of enforcement of irreconcilable judgments given in different Contracting States.

In the *Gabriel* case decided on 11 July 2002, the Court delivered a judgment on Article 13(1) point 3 of the Convention on jurisdiction in matters relating to consumers' contracts in a dispute on the entitlement of a consumer to a prize apparently won after a misleading advertisement. The judgment issued on 17 September 2002, in *Fonderie Officine Meccaniche Tacconi*, concerned the interpretation of Article 5(1) and the concept of pre-contractual liability.

In the *Henkel* case, in a judgment delivered on 1 October 2002, the Court interpreted Article 5(3) on jurisdiction in matters relating to tort, delict or quasi-delict.

The final judgment delivered in 2002, in the *Baten* case, issued on 14 November, the Court interpreted Article 1 of the Convention and more specifically the concepts of "civil and commercial matters" and "social security".

Thirteen cases are still pending before the Court at the end of 2002. In three cases, opinions of the Advocates Generals have already been delivered and judgments of the Court are to be expected in the earlier months of 2003. This supplement is therefore only the first one. More supplements will no doubt follow to keep up to date with the case law of the European Court of Justice on jurisdiction and enforcement of judgments in civil and commercial matters.

Paolo Galizzi

17 December 2002

Case C-518/99 - 5 April 2001

Richard Gaillard
v
Alaya Chekili

Article 104(3) of the Rules of Procedure - Article 16(1) - Exclusive jurisdiction in proceedings which have as their object rights in rem in immovable property - Scope - Action for rescission of a contract of sale of immovable property and for damages

ORDER OF THE COURT (Sixth Chamber)

Gulmann, President of the Chamber, Skouris, Puissochet, Schintgen (Rapporteur) and Colneric, Judges

1. By judgment of 22 December 1999, received at the Court on 31 December 1999, the Cour d'Appel de Bruxelles, in Belgium, referred to the Court for a preliminary ruling, pursuant to the Protocol of 3 June 1971 on the interpretation by the Court of Justice of the Convention of 27 September 1968 on jurisdiction and the enforcement of judgments in civil and commercial matters a question on the interpretation of Article 16(1) of that Convention (OJ 1978 L 304, p. 36), as amended by the Convention of 9 October 1978 on the accession of the Kingdom of Denmark, Ireland and the United Kingdom of Great Britain and Northern Ireland (OJ 1978 L 304, p. 1 - see p. 77 for the amended text) and by the Convention of 25 October 1982 on the accession of the Hellenic Republic (OJ 1982 L 388, p. 1, hereinafter 'the Brussels Convention).

2. This question was raised in proceedings brought by Mr Gaillard against Mr Chekili concerning a contract for the sale of several immovable properties located in France.

The Brussels Convention

3. The first paragraph of Article 2 of the Brussels Convention, which is comprised in Section 1, headed 'General Provisions', of Title II, relating to 'Jurisdiction, provides:

'[S]ubject to the provisions of this Convention, persons domiciled in a Contracting State shall, whatever their nationality, be sued in the courts of that State.'

4. Article 16, which forms Section 5, headed 'Exclusive Jurisdiction, of Title II of the Convention', states:

'[T]he following courts shall have exclusive jurisdiction, regardless of domicile:

1. in proceedings which have as their object rights *in rem* in, or tenancies of, immovable property, the courts of the Contracting State in which the property is situated';

...

5. According to Article 12(1) of the Convention of 25 October 1982:

'[T]he 1968 Convention and the 1971 Protocol, as amended by the 1978 Convention and this Convention, shall apply only to legal proceedings instituted ... after the entry into force of this Convention in the State of origin ...'

6. The Convention of 25 October 1982 entered into force in Belgium on 1 April 1989.

The main proceedings

7. The file relating to the main proceedings shows that by a contract of sale of 4 October 1991 Mr Gaillard sold to Mr Chekili two properties and a number of plots of land situated in France for an aggregate sum of BEF 30 000 000. On the same day, the purchaser paid to the seller a deposit of 10% of the sale price. Under the general conditions of the contract, the officially attested instrument of sale was to be signed no later than four months after the conclusion of the contract.

8. As the officially attested instrument of sale had none the less not been executed pursuant to the contract, by summons to appear before the Tribunal de Première Instance de Bruxelles, Belgium, of 14 December 1992, Mr Gaillard brought proceedings against Mr Chekili for rescission of the contract of sale and for damages in accordance with the general

conditions of the contract of sale entered into by the parties. Those conditions provide, on the one hand, that if one of the parties is in default in the performance of his contractual obligations, and is served with a formal notice which is not complied with within a period of 15 days following service, the other party may seek either specific performance of the contract or rescission of the sale, with the sums paid by way of deposit remaining with the seller where the purchaser is in default, and, on the other hand, that in cases of late payment, the purchaser must pay interest to the seller at an annual rate of 10% on the amount remaining due.

9. That court having declined jurisdiction by reason of Article 16(1) of the Brussels Convention, on the grounds that the properties that were the subject of the contract of sale were situated in France, Mr Gaillard appealed to the Cour d'Appel de Bruxelles which decided to stay proceedings and to refer the following question to the Court for a preliminary ruling:

'Does an action for rescission of a contract for the sale of land and consequential damages amount to proceedings which have as their object rights *in rem* of immovable property within the meaning of Article 16 of the Convention of 27 September 1968 between the Member States of the European Economic Community on jurisdiction and the enforcement of judgments in civil and commercial matters, signed in Brussels on 27 September 1968?'

The question referred for a preliminary ruling

10. By this question, the national court asks in substance whether the action for rescission of a contract of sale relating to immovable property and for consequential damages falls within the scope of the rule on exclusive jurisdiction in proceedings having as their object rights *in rem* of immovable property laid down by Article 16(1) of the Brussels Convention.

11. Considering that, in the light of the Court's settled case-law, the answer to that question admits of no reasonable doubt, the Court informed the national court pursuant to Article 104(3) of its Rules of Procedure that it proposed to give its decision by reasoned order and invited the Member States together with the other persons referred to in Article 20 of the EC Statute of the Court of Justice to submit any observations they might have on that proposal.

12. Mr Gaillard, the German Government and the Commission made

no objection to the Court's proposal to give its decision by reasoned order. However, the Spanish Government expressed a contrary view.

13. For the purpose of deciding the question referred for a preliminary ruling, it must first be observed that it follows from settled case-law that in order to ensure that the rights and obligations arising out of the Brussels Convention for the Contracting States and for individuals concerned are as equal and uniform as possible, an independent definition must be given in Community law to the phrase 'in proceedings which have as their object rights *in rem* in immovable property within the meaning of Article 16(1) of the Convention' (see, in particular, the judgment in Case C-115/88 *Reichert and Kockler* [1990] ECR I-27, paragraph 8).

14. Next, the Court has repeatedly held that Article 16 of the Brussels Convention, being an exception to the general rule of jurisdiction set out in the first paragraph of Article 2 of the Convention, must not be given a wider interpretation than that required by its objective, given that it results in depriving the parties of the choice of forum which would otherwise be theirs and, in certain cases, results in their being brought before a court which is not that of the domicile of any of them (see the judgments in Cases 73/77 *Sanders* [1977] ECR 2383, paragraphs 17 and 18, *Reichert and Kockler,* paragraph 9, C-292/93 *Lieber* [1994] ECR I-2535, paragraph 12, and C-8/98 *Dansommer* [2000] ECR I-393, paragraph 21).

15. In those circumstances, the Court has held that Article 16(1) of the Brussels Convention must be interpreted as meaning that the exclusive jurisdiction of the Contracting State in which the property is situated does not encompass all actions concerning rights *in rem* in immovable property but only those which both come within the scope of the Brussels Convention and are actions which seek to determine the extent, content, ownership or possession of immovable property or the existence of other rights *in rem* therein and to provide the holders of those rights with the protection of the powers which attach to their interest (see the judgment in *Reichert and Kockler,* paragraph 11).

16. It is also settled case-law that it is not sufficient, for Article 16(1) to apply, that a right *in rem* in immovable property be involved in the action or that the action has a link with immovable property. On the contrary, the action must be based on a right *in rem* and not on a right *in personam,* save in the case of the exception concerning tenancies of immovable property (see the judgments in C-294/92 *Webb* [1994] ECR I-1717, paragraph 14, *Lieber,* paragraph 13, and *Dansommer,* paragraph 22).

17. In this regard, it is clear from the Schlosser Report on the association of the Kingdom of Denmark, Ireland and the United Kingdom of Great Britain and Northern Ireland to the Convention on jurisdiction and the enforcement of judgments in civil and commercial matters and to the Protocol on its interpretation by the Court of Justice (OJ 1979 C 59, p. 71, at p. 120, hereinafter 'the Schlosser Report) that the difference between a right *in rem* and a right *in personam* is that the former, existing in an item of property, has effect *erga omnes*, whereas the latter can only be claimed against the debtor (see the judgment in *Lieber,* paragraph 14).

18. Even if, in some circumstances, proceedings for rescission of a contract for the sale of immovable property may have some impact on the title to the property, they are none the less based on the personal right that the claimant obtains under the contract entered into between the parties and consequently may only be raised against the other party to the contract. By raising these proceedings, one party to the contract seeks to be released from his contractual obligations towards the other party, by reason of the latter's failure to perform the contract. Furthermore, the decision of the court which is to decide the case is capable of having effect only as regards the party against whom the order of rescission is made. It follows that the proceedings do not have as their object rights which relate directly to immovable property and can be raised *erga omnes*.

19. It follows that the action for rescission in the main proceedings does not constitute proceedings which have as their object rights *in rem* in immovable property within the meaning of Article 16(1) of the Brussels Convention, but is an action *in personam*.

20. The same applies to the claim for damages which seeks compensation for the harm alleged by one party to have been suffered by it as a result of the rescission of a contract for the sale of immovable property by reason of the other party to the contract's failure to perform its contractual obligations (see also the Schlosser Report, p. 120, and the judgment in *Lieber*).

21. That interpretation is moreover confirmed by the Schlosser Report (p. 122) which states that in the case of mixed actions, such as an action for restitution of property raised by a party where the other party to the contract is not performing his obligations under the contract for sale of the property, there are numerous factors which support the view that such actions are predominantly actions *in personam* and that accordingly Article 16(1) of the Brussels Convention does not apply.

22. It follows that the answer to the question referred to is that an action for rescission of a contract for the sale of land and consequential damages is not within the scope of the rules on exclusive jurisdiction in proceedings which have as their object rights *in rem* in immovable property under Article 16(1) of the Brussels Convention.

On those grounds,

THE COURT (Sixth Chamber),

in answer to the question referred to it by the Cour d'Appel de Bruxelles by judgment of 22 December 1999, hereby rules:

> **An action for rescission of a contract for the sale of land and consequential damages is not within the scope of the rules on exclusive jurisdiction in proceedings which have as their object rights *in rem* in immovable property under Article 16(1) of the Convention of 27 September 1968 between the Member States of the European Economic Community on jurisdiction and the enforcement of judgments in civil and commercial matters, as amended by the Convention of 9 October 1978 on the accession of the Kingdom of Denmark, Ireland and the United Kingdom of Great Britain and Northern Ireland and by the Convention of 25 October 1982 on the accession of the Hellenic Republic.**

Case C-256/00 - 19 February 2002

Besix SA
v
Wasserreinigungsbau Alfred Kretzschmar GmbH & Co. KG (WABAG)

Planungs- und Forschungsgesellschaft Dipl. Ing. W. Kretzschmar GmbH & Co. KG (Plafog)

Article 5(1) - Jurisdiction in matters relating to a contract - Place of performance of the obligation in question - Obligation not to do something, applicable without geographical limit - Undertakings given by two companies not to bind themselves to other partners when tendering for a public contract - Application of Article 2

JUDGMENT OF THE COURT

Rodríguez Iglesias, President, Jann, Macken and Colneric (Presidents of Chambers), La Pergola, Puissochet, Wathelet, Schintgen (Rapporteur) and Skouris, Judges,

1. By judgment of 19 June 2000, received at the Court on 28 June 2000, the Cour d'Appel de Bruxelles (Court of Appeal, Brussels) referred to the Court for a preliminary ruling under the Protocol of 3 June 1971 on the interpretation by the Court of Justice of the Convention of 27 September 1968 on Jurisdiction and the Enforcement of Judgments in Civil and Commercial Matters a question on the interpretation of Article 5(1) of that Convention (OJ 1978 L 304, p. 36), as amended by the Convention of 9 October 1978 on the Accession of the Kingdom of Denmark, Ireland and the United Kingdom of Great Britain and Northern Ireland (OJ 1978 L 304, p. 1 - amended version - p. 77, hereinafter 'the Brussels Convention').

2. That question has been raised in proceedings between the Belgian company Besix SA (hereinafter 'Besix'), established at Brussels (Belgium) and the German companies Wasserreinigungsbau Alfred Kretzschmar GmbH & Co. KG (hereinafter 'WABAG') and Planungs- und Forschungsgellschaft Dipl. Ing. W. Kretzschmar GmbH & Co. KG (hereinafter 'Plafog'), both established at Kulmbach (Germany), concerning a claim for damages lodged by Besix against WABAG and Plafog for loss which it alleges it suffered owing to breach by those two companies of an exclusivity clause in the context of a contract concerning a public invitation to tender.

The Brussels Convention

3. The jurisdiction rules laid down by the Brussels Convention are contained in Title II, which consists of Articles 2 to 24.

4. In this regard, the first paragraph of Article 2 of the Brussels Convention, which forms part of Section 1, entitled 'General provisions', of Title II, states:

'Subject to the provisions of this Convention, persons domiciled in a Contracting State shall, whatever their nationality, be sued in the courts of that State.'

5. The first paragraph of Article 3 of the Brussels Convention, which is in the same section, provides:

'Persons domiciled in a Contracting State may be sued in the courts of another Contracting State only by virtue of the rules set out in Sections 2 to 6 of this title.'

6. Thus, under Article 5, which is part of Section 2, entitled 'Special jurisdiction', of Title II of the Brussels Convention:

'A person domiciled in a Contracting State may, in another Contracting State, be sued:

(1) in matters relating to a contract, in the courts for the place of performance of the obligation in question;

...'

The main proceedings and the question referred for a preliminary ruling

7. According to the national court's case-file, on 24 January 1984, WABAG, which belongs to the Deutsche Babcock group, and Besix signed in Brussels an agreement drawn up in French whereby they undertook to submit a joint tender in response to a public invitation to tender

for a project of the 'Ministry of Mines and Energy of Cameroon' called 'water supply in 11 urban centres in Cameroon' and, if their tender were accepted, to perform the contract jointly.

8. Under the terms of the agreement, the two companies undertook 'to act exclusively and not to commit themselves to other partners'.

9. However, when the tenders were opened, it was found that Plafog, which, like WABAG, is part of the Deutsche Babcock group, had, in association with a Finnish undertaking, also taken part in the tender for the public contract in question.

10. After all the tenders had been assessed, it was decided to split the contract and to entrust different lots to different undertakings. One lot was awarded to the group which included Plafog whilst the WABAG-Besix group, which was lower placed, did not win any part of the contract.

11. Besix, taking the view that the exclusivity and non-competition clause had been breached, brought an action in damages against WABAG and Plafog on 19 August 1987 before the Tribunal de Commerce de Bruxelles claiming damages of BEF 80 000 000.

12. That court found that it had jurisdiction to hear Besix's claim pursuant to Article 5(1) of the Brussels Convention on the ground that, under the conflict rule of the court before which the matter had been brought, the applicable law was that of the State with which the contract had the closest connection and that the obligation in question, namely the exclusivity undertaking, should have been performed in Belgium as a corollary to the preparation of the joint tender.

13. When, however, its action was dismissed as unfounded, Besix took its case to the Cour d'Appel de Bruxelles.

14. By way of cross appeal, WABAG and Plafog contended that only the German courts had jurisdiction to hear and determine the case.

15. Besix, on the other hand, submitted that the obligation of exclusivity had been partially performed in Belgium, since the non-competition undertaking enabled the joint tender to be prepared and that fact alone was sufficient to confer jurisdiction on the Belgian courts, under Article 5(1) of the Brussels Convention.

16. According to the Cour d'Appel, the contractual obligation in question, as referred to in Article 5(1) of the Brussels Convention, consists in the present case of the undertaking - which, according to Besix, was breached by WABAG and Plafog - to act exclusively and without commitment to other partners in relation to the public contract in question.

17. Having regard to the line of case-law beginning with the judgment of 6 October 1976 in Case 12/76 *Tessili* [1976] ECR 1473, according to which the place of performance of the obligation in question must be determined in accordance to the law governing that obligation as designated by the rules on the conflict of laws of the court before which the matter is brought, and with regard to the fact that the Convention on the Law applicable to Contractual Obligations opened for signature in Rome in 19 June 1980 (OJ 1980 L 266, p. 1), is not applicable in the present case - since the Belgian ratification law limited its application to contracts concluded after 1 January 1988 - Belgian private international law designates, according to the Cour d'Appel, as the law applicable to the contract (unless the parties have chosen the applicable law, which was not the case here), the law of the country with which the contract has the closest connection.

18. The agreement of 24 January 1984 was concluded in Brussels. Furthermore, Besix, which was responsible for the greater part of the contract, was regarded as the leader of the WABAG-Besix group and was centralising operations in Brussels with a view to preparing the joint tender. Consequently, Belgian law, according to the Cour d'Appel, is the law of the country with which the contract, including the exclusivity undertaking which it contained, had the closest connection.

19. Belgium was also the place where the parties had in fact the greatest interest in honouring their undertaking to act exclusively, since it was in that Contracting State that they were to prepare the joint tender and, more generally, there is in this case a particularly close connecting factor between the present dispute and the Belgian courts such as to render Article 5(1) of the Brussels Convention applicable.

20. However, the Cour d'Appel raises the question of whether the fact that the undertaking to act exclusively was to be honoured, *inter alia*, in Belgium - and was indeed honoured in Belgium, since it was in Germany that Plafog negotiated with the Finnish undertaking - is sufficient to confer jurisdiction on the Belgian courts. Since the parties' undoubted intention was that the other contracting party should not commit itself to

another partner for the purpose of submitting a joint tender for the public contract concerned, the place where any such commitment was entered into or fulfilled does not matter and the exclusivity obligation in question was applicable in any place whatever in the world, the places for performance of that obligation therefore being particularly numerous.

21. Taking the view that, in those circumstances, determination of the case required an interpretation of the Brussels Convention, the Cour d'Appel de Bruxelles decided to stay proceedings and to refer the following question to the Court for a preliminary ruling:

'Must Article 5(1) of the [Brussels] Convention ... be interpreted as meaning that a defendant domiciled in a Contracting State may, in another Contracting State, be sued, in matters relating to a contract, in the courts for any of the places of performance of the obligation in question, in particular where, consisting in an obligation not to do something - such as, in the present case, an undertaking to act exclusively with another party to a contract with a view to submitting a joint bid for a public contract and not to enter into a commitment with another partner - that obligation is to be performed in any place whatever in the world?

If not, may that defendant be sued specifically in the courts for one of the places of performance of the obligation and, if so, by reference to what criterion must that place be determined?'

22. It is clear from the order for reference that the Cour d'Appel de Bruxelles found, first, that the relevant obligation for the purposes of the application of Article 5(1) of the Brussels Convention was an obligation not to do something, consisting here in 'the parties' undertaking not to commit themselves to other partners in connection with a procedure for the award of a public contract, and, second, that the parties did not designate either the place of performance of that contractual obligation or the courts having jurisdiction to hear any action relating to such an obligation, or, for that matter, the law governing the contract. The referring court also states that, given all the circumstances of the case, 'the parties' clear intention was to have the obligation in question honoured throughout the world, with the result that the places for its performance are particularly numerous.

23. The question referred for a preliminary ruling must be answered in the light of those factors.

24. As the referring court itself points out, the Court has repeatedly held that the principle of legal certainty is one of the objectives of the Brussels

Convention (Case 38/81 *Effer* [1982] ECR 825, paragraph 6; Case C-26/91 *Handte* [1992] ECR I-3967, paragraphs 11, 12, 18 and 19; Case C-129/92 *Owens Bank* [1994] ECR I-117, paragraph 32; Case C-288/92 *Custom Made Commercial* [1994] ECR I-2913, paragraph 18; and Case C-440/97 *GIE Groupe Concorde and Others* [1999] ECR I-6307, paragraph 23).

25. According to its preamble, the Brussels Convention is intended to strengthen in the Community the legal protection of persons established therein, by laying down common rules on jurisdiction to guarantee certainty as to the allocation of jurisdiction among the various national courts before which proceedings in a particular case may be brought (see, to that effect, *Custom Made Commercial*, cited above, paragraph 15).

26. That principle of legal certainty requires, in particular, that the jurisdictional rules which derogate from the basic principle of the Brussels Convention laid down in Article 2, such as the rule in Article 5(1), should be interpreted in such a way as to enable a normally well-informed defendant reasonably to foresee before which courts, other than those of the State in which he is domiciled, he may be sued (*Handte*, cited above, paragraph 18, and *GIE Groupe Concorde and Others*, paragraph 24).

27. Second, the Court has consistently held that it is essential to avoid, so far as possible, creating a situation in which a number of courts have jurisdiction in respect of one and the same contract, in order to preclude the risk of irreconcilable decisions and to facilitate the recognition and enforcement of judgments in States other than those in which they were delivered (Case 14/76 *De Bloos* [1976] ECR 1497, paragraph 9; Case 266/85 *Shenavai* [1987] ECR 239, paragraph 8; Case C-125/92 *Mulox IBC* [1993] ECR I-4075, paragraph 21; Case C-383/95 *Rutten* [1997] ECR I-57, paragraph 18; and Case C-420/97 *Leathertex* [1999] ECR I-6747, paragraph 31).

28. It follows from the foregoing that Article 5(1) of the Brussels Convention is to be interpreted as meaning that, in the event that the relevant contractual obligation has been, or is to be, performed in a number of places, jurisdiction to hear and determine the case cannot be conferred on the court within whose jurisdiction any one of those places of performance happens to be located.

29. Rather, as is clear from the very wording of that provision, which,

in matters relating to a contract, confers jurisdiction on the courts 'for the place of performance of the obligation in question, a single place of performance for the obligation in question must be identified'.

30. According to the Jenard Report on the Brussels Convention (OJ 1979 C 59, p. 1, at p. 22), the special rules of jurisdiction laid down in Section 2 of Title II of that Convention are justified in particular by the consideration that there is a close connecting factor between the dispute and the court called upon to resolve it (see Case 56/79 *Zelger* [1980] ECR 89, paragraph 3).

31. The reason for the adoption of the jurisdictional rule in Article 5(1) of the Brussels Convention was concern for sound administration of justice and efficacious conduct of proceedings (see, to this effect, in particular *Tessili*, paragraph 13; *Shenavai*, paragraph 6, and *Mulox IBC*, paragraph 17, and, by way of analogy, as regards Article 5(3) of the Brussels Convention, Case C-220/88 *Dumez France and Tracoba* [1990] ECR I-49, paragraph 17; Case C-68/93 *Shevill and Others* [1995] ECR I-415, paragraph 19; and Case C-364/93 *Marinari* [1995] ECR I-2719, paragraph 10). The court of the place where the contractual obligation giving rise to the action is to be performed will normally be the most appropriate for deciding the case, in particular on the grounds of proximity and ease of taking evidence.

32. It follows that, in a case such as that now referred, characterised by a multiplicity of places of performance of the contractual obligation in question, a single place of performance has to be identified. In principle, this will be the place presenting the closest connection between the dispute and the court having jurisdiction.

33. However, as the Commission rightly points out, application of the Court's traditional case-law, according to which the place of the performance of the obligation in question, within the meaning of Article 5(1) of the Brussels Convention, is to be determined in accordance with the law governing the obligation in question, according to the conflict rules of the court seised (*Tessili*, paragraphs 13 and 15; *Custom Made Commercial*, paragraph 26; *GIE Groupe Concorde and Others*, paragraph 32; and *Leathertex*, paragraph 33), does not enable that result to be achieved.

34. Where parties have agreed a contractual obligation not to do something, applicable without any geographical limit, that approach does not

avoid a multiplicity of competent courts, since it leads to the result that the places of performance of the obligation in question are in all the Contracting States. It also involves the risk that the claimant will be able to choose the place of performance which he judges to be most favourable to his interests.

35. Consequently, that interpretation does not make it possible to identify the court most qualified territorially to determine the case. Furthermore, it is likely to reduce the predictability of the competent court, so that it is incompatible with the principle of legal certainty.

36. A further point is that it is not possible, in a situation such as that at issue in the present case, to give an autonomous interpretation of the place of performance, referred to in Article 5(1) of the Brussels Convention, without calling in question the case-law established since *Tessili*, recalled in paragraph 33 above and upheld most recently by the Court in its judgments in *GIE Groupe Concorde and Others* and *Leathertex.*

37. Accordingly, contrary to the approach envisaged by the court which has referred this case, the place of performance of the obligation in question in the present case cannot be identified on the basis of factual considerations, that is, on the basis of the specific circumstances of the case evidencing a particularly close connection between the case and a Contracting State.

38. Further, it is true that there is settled case-law, as regards contracts of employment, to the effect, first, that the place of performance of the relevant obligation should be determined by reference, not to the applicable national law in accordance with the conflict rules of the court seised, but to uniform criteria which it is for the Court to lay down on the basis of the scheme and objectives of the Brussels Convention (*Mulox IBC*, paragraph 16); next, that those criteria lead to the choice of the place where the employee actually performs the work covered by the contract with his employer (*Mulox IBC*, paragraph 20); finally, that, where the employee performs his work in more than one Contracting State, the place where the obligation characterising the contract is to be performed, within the meaning of Article 5(1) of the Brussels Convention, is theplace where or from which the employee principally discharges his obligations towards his employer (*Mulox IBC*, paragraph 26) or where the employee has established the effective centre of his activities (*Rutten*, paragraph 26).

39. However, contrary to the alternative argument put forward by Besix, that case-law of the Court, rehearsed in the preceding paragraph, cannot be applied by analogy in the present case.

40. As the Court has repeatedly held (see, in particular, *Shenavai*, paragraph 17, *GIE Groupe Concorde and Others*, paragraph 19, and *Leathertex*, paragraph 36), where these specific features of a contract of employment are lacking, it is neither necessary nor appropriate to identify the obligation which characterises the contract and to centralise at its place of performance all jurisdiction, based on place of performance, over disputes concerning all the obligations under the contract.

41. As for the solution consisting in choosing as the place of performance the place where the breach of the obligation in question was committed, that cannot be applied either, since it would also imply a reversal of the *Tessili* case-law, by giving an autonomous interpretation to the concept of place of performance, without looking at the law applicable to the relevant obligation in accordance with the conflict rules of the court seised. Besides, it would not avoid the situation of many courts having jurisdiction in the event that that obligation had not been honoured in many different Contracting States.

42. Finally, the Commission proposes to apply by analogy the solution adopted by the Court in paragraph 19 of the judgment in *Shenavai*, so that, for the purposes of Article 5(1) of the Brussels Convention, the determining factor, in a case such as this, would not be the place of performance of the non-competition undertaking but the place of performance of the positive obligation to which that undertaking is accessory, in that it guarantees its proper performance.

43. Besix has suggested a variant of that solution, whereby the negative obligation in question in the instant case should be regarded as the corollary of the obligation, arising from the agreement concluded on 24 January 1984 between Besix and WABAG, to participate in submitting a tender for the public contract in question and to perform the works put out to tender, so that it would be the place of performance of that latter obligation which should be determined.

44. The Court finds, however, that such an interpretation would be hardly compatible with the wording of Article 5(1) of the Brussels Convention, which, since its amendment, in some language versions, by the Convention of 9 October 1978 on the Accession of the Kingdom of

Denmark, Ireland and the United Kingdom of Great Britain and Northern Ireland, specifies that the obligation whose place of performance determines which court has jurisdiction is 'the obligation which forms the basis of the claim [in the English version 'the obligation in question]. Nor would that interpretation becompatible with the case-law of the Court on the version prior to that amendment of that provision, according to which the obligation whose place of performance determines judicial jurisdiction for the purposes of Article 5(1) is that which arises under the contract and the non-performance of which is relied upon in support of the action (*De Bloos*, paragraphs 14 and 15).

45. In the present case, as may be seen from paragraph 16 of this judgment, the national court found that only the obligation of exclusivity and non-competition was in question, the sole purpose of the legal action brought by Besix being to obtain compensation for the damage which it claims to have suffered through breach of that obligation by WABAG and Plafog. Accordingly, the question referred by the Cour d'Appel de Bruxelles relates solely to determination of the place for performance of that negative obligation. However, the approach advocated by Besix and the Commission would entail the prior determination of the relevant positive obligation.

46. It is, moreover, settled case-law that, in view of the allocation of jurisdiction under the preliminary ruling procedure provided for by the Protocol of 3 June 1971 on the interpretation of the Brussels Convention by the Court of Justice, it is for the national court to rule on those questions of fact, the Court confining itself to interpreting that Convention in the light of the findings made by the national court (see, to that effect, *Leathertex*, paragraph 21).

47. Further, unlike the situation in the case now before the court making this reference, the dispute which led to the ruling in *Shenavai* concerned two distinct obligations.

48. In view of the considerations set forth above, it appears that Article 5(1) of the Brussels Convention is not apt to apply in a case such as that in the main proceedings, where it is not possible to determine the court having the closest connection with the case by making jurisdiction coincide with the actual place for performance of the obligation considered relevant by the national court.

49. By its very nature, an obligation not to do something, which, like

that in question in the main proceedings, consists in an undertaking to act exclusively with a contracting partner and a prohibition restraining those parties from committing themselves to another partner for the purpose of submitting a joint tender for a public contract and which, according to the parties' intention, is applicable without any geographical limit and must therefore be honoured throughout the world - and, in particular, in each of the Contracting States—, is not capable of being identified with a specific place or linked to a court which would be particularly suited to hear and determine the dispute relating to that obligation. By definition, such an undertaking to refrain from doing something in any place whatsoever is not linked to any particular court rather than to any other.

50. In those circumstances jurisdiction can, in such a case, be determined solely in accordance with Article 2 of the Brussels Convention, which provides a certain and reliable criterion (Case 32/88 *Six Constructions* [1989] ECR 341, paragraph 20).

51. That solution is, moreover, in conformity with the scheme of the Brussels Convention and the rationale of Article 5(1) thereof.

52. The system of common rules on conferment of jurisdiction laid down in Title II of the Brussels Convention is based on the general rule, set out in the first paragraph of Article 2, that persons domiciled in a Contracting State are to be sued in the courts of that State, irrespective of the nationality of the parties. That jurisdictional rule is a general principle, which expresses the maxim *actor sequitur forum rei*, because it makes it easier, in principle, for a defendant to defend himself (see, in particular, Case C-412/98 *Group Josi* [2000] ECR I-5925, paragraphs 34 and 35).

53. It is only by way of derogation from that fundamental principle that the Brussels Convention makes provision, in accordance with the first paragraph of Article 3, for, in particular, special jurisdictional rules, such as that laid down in Article 5(1), where the choice depends on an option to be exercised by the claimant.

54. However, it is well settled that that option must not give rise to an interpretation going beyond the cases expressly envisaged by the Brussels Convention, for otherwise the general principle laid down in the first paragraph of Article 2 would be undermined and a claimant might be able to affect the choice of a court unforeseeable for a defendant domiciled in the territory of a Contracting State (see, in particular, *Group Josi*, paragraphs 49 and 50, and the references there).

55. In the light of all the foregoing considerations, the answer to be given to the question referred for a preliminary ruling must be that the special jurisdictional rule in matters relating to a contract laid down in Article 5(1) of the Brussels Convention is not applicable where, as in the present case, the place of performance of the obligation in question cannot be determined because it consists in an undertaking not to do something which is not subject to any geographical limit and is therefore characterised by a multiplicity of places for its performance. In such a case, jurisdiction can be determined only by application of the general criterion laid down in the first paragraph of Article 2 of the Convention.

On those grounds,

THE COURT,

in answer to the question referred to it by the Cour d'Appel de Bruxelles by judgment of 19 June 2000, hereby rules:

> **The special jurisdictional rule in matters relating to a contract, laid down in Article 5(1) of the Convention of 27 September 1968 on Jurisdiction and the Enforcement of Judgments in Civil and Commercial Matters, as amended by the Convention of 9 October 1978 on the Accession of the Kingdom of Denmark, Ireland and the United Kingdom of Great Britain and Northern Ireland, is not applicable where, as in the present case, the place of performance of the obligation in question cannot be determined because it consists in an undertaking not to do something which is not subject to any geographical limit and is therefore characterised by a multiplicity of places for its performance. In such a case, jurisdiction can be determined only by application of the general criterion laid down in the first paragraph of Article 2 of that Convention.**

Case C-37/00 - 27 February 2002

Herbert Weber
v
Universal Ogden Services Ltd

Article 5(1) - Courts for the place of performance of the contractual obligation - Contract of employment - Place where the employee habitually carries out his work - Definition - Work performed partly at an installation positioned over the continental shelf adjacent to a Contracting State and partly in the territory of another Contracting State

JUDGMENT OF THE COURT (Sixth Chamber)

Macken, President of the Chamber, Colneric, Puissochet, Schintgen (Rapporteur) and Skouris, Judges

1. By judgment of 4 February 2000, received at the Court on 10 February 2000, the Hoge Raad der Nederlanden (Supreme Court of the Netherlands) referred to the Court for a preliminary ruling under the Protocol of 3 June 1971 on the interpretation by the Court of Justice of the Convention of 27 September 1968 on Jurisdiction and the Enforcement of Judgments in Civil and Commercial Matters (OJ 1978 L 304, p. 36) three questions on the interpretation of Article 5(1) of that convention, as amended by the Convention of 9 October 1978 on the Accession of the Kingdom of Denmark, Ireland and the United Kingdom of Great Britain and Northern Ireland (OJ 1978 L 304, p. 1 and - amended version - p. 77), by the Convention of 25 October 1982 on the Accession of the Hellenic Republic (OJ 1982 L 388, p. 1) and by the Convention of 26 May 1989 on the Accession of the Kingdom of Spain and the Portuguese Republic (OJ 1989 L 285, p. 1) (hereinafter 'the Brussels Convention').

2. Those questions were raised in proceedings between Mr Weber, a German national residing in Krefeld (Germany), and his employer Universal Ogden Services Ltd (hereinafter 'UOS'), a company incorporated under Scottish law and established in Aberdeen (United Kingdom), following the termination of Mr Weber's contract of employment by UOS.

Relevant law

The Brussels Convention

3. The rules on jurisdiction laid down by the Brussels Convention are to be found in Title II thereof, which contains Articles 2 to 24.

4. The first paragraph of Article 2 of the Brussels Convention, which forms part of Section 1, entitled 'General provisions', of Title II, states:

'Subject to the provisions of this convention, persons domiciled in a Contracting State shall, whatever their nationality, be sued in the courts of that State.'

5. The first paragraph of Article 3 of the Brussels Convention, which appears in the same section, provides:

'Persons domiciled in a Contracting State may be sued in the courts of another Contracting State only by virtue of the rules set out in Sections 2 to 6 of this title.'

6. In Sections 2 to 6 of Title II, the Brussels Convention lays down rules on special or exclusive jurisdiction.

7. Thus, under Article 5, which appears in Section 2, entitled 'Special jurisdiction', of Title II of the Brussels Convention:

'A person domiciled in a Contracting State may, in another Contracting State, be sued:

1. In matters relating to a contract, in the courts for the place of performance of the obligation in question; in matters relating to individual contracts of employment, this place is that where the employee habitually carries out his work, or if the employee does not habitually carry out his work in any one country, the employer may also be sued in the courts for the place where the business which engaged the employee was or is now situated;

...'.

Applicable international law

8. The Convention on the Continental Shelf, concluded in Geneva on 29 April 1958 (hereinafter 'the Geneva Convention') came into force on 10 June 1964 and was ratified by the Kingdom of the Netherlands on 18 February 1996. The United Nations Convention on the Law of the Sea, signed in Montego Bay on 10 December 1982, on the other hand, was not ratified by the Kingdom of the Netherlands until 28 June 1996 and consequently was not applicable in that State at the material time.

The relevant national provisions

9. In the Netherlands, the Wet arbeid mijnbouw Noordzee (Law relating to Employment in Extraction Industries in the North Sea, hereinafter 'the WAMN') of 2 November 1992 entered into force on 1 February 1993.

10. Article 1(a) of the WAMN provides that, for the purposes of that law, the 'continental shelf' has the same meaning as in the Mijnwet continentaal plat (Law on Mining on the Continental Shelf) of 23 September 1965, that is to say that part of the seabed and substratum situated below the North Sea outside the territorial waters over which the Kingdom of the Netherlands exercises sovereign rights, in particular under the Geneva Convention (hereinafter 'the Netherlands continental shelf').

11. Under Article 1(b) of the WAMN the term 'mining installation' means, for the purposes of that law, an installation positioned on or above the Netherlands continental shelf for the purposes of prospecting or extracting minerals, or a group of installations of which at least one fits that description.

12. It is clear from the explanatory notes to Article 1 of the WAMN that that definition of mining installation also includes drilling vessels and all mineral prospecting or extracting installations situated outside territorial waters, whether they be fixed or (immobilised) floating installations.

13. Article 1(c) of the WAMN provides that, for the purposes of that law, 'employee' means:

'1. a person who works on or from a mining installation under a contract of employment;

2. a person, other than a person referred to in subparagraph 1, engaged under a contract of employment for a period of at least 30 days to carry out charting or mineral prospecting or mining work on or from a ship situated within territorial waters or above the continental shelf under the North Sea outside territorial waters'.

14. Article 2 of the WAMN is worded as follows:

'Employees' contracts of employment are governed by the Netherlands law of employment contracts and any rules of private international law relating thereto. For the purposes of applying rules of private international law, work carried out by an employee is deemed to have been carried out in the territory of the Netherlands.'

15. Article 10(1) of the WAMN provides:

'Subject to Articles 98(2) and 126 of the Code of Civil Procedure, the Kantonrechter te Alkmaar shall have jurisdiction in disputes concerning 'employees' contracts of employment and concerning the application of this Law.'

16. The explanatory notes to Article 10 of the WAMN stipulate that that provision does not derogate from the rules laid down in the Brussels Convention.

The main proceedings and the questions referred

17. It is apparent from the case-file in the main proceedings that, from July 1987 to 30 December 1993, Mr Weber was employed by UOS as a cook.

18. The national court observes that, until 21 September 1993, part of Mr Weber's work for UOS was carried out on board mining vessels or on mining installations covered by the WAMN and stationed over the Netherlands continental shelf.

19. According to the national court, precisely when, during the period between the commencement of his employment relationship with UOS in July 1987 and 21 September 1993, Mr Weber worked in the Netherlands continental shelf area has not been established; nor have the exact dates on which he worked on mining installations or vessels covered by the WAMN.

20. Mr Weber in fact alleges that, during that period, he worked principally in the Netherlands continental shelf area on mining installations and ships flying the Dutch flag. UOS, however, disputes the accuracy of that assertion.

21. On the other hand, it is common ground that, from 21 September to 30 December 1993, Mr Weber worked as a cook on board a floating crane deployed in Danish territorial waters for the construction of a bridge over the Great Belt (Denmark).

22. On 29 June 1994 Mr Weber brought an action against UOS before the Kantonrechter (Cantonal Court) te Alkmaar (Netherlands), in accordance with Article 10(1) of the WAMN, alleging that the company had terminated his employment unlawfully.

23. That court dismissed, on the basis of Netherlands law, a plea of lack of jurisdiction raised by UOS and held part of Mr Weber's action to be well founded.

24. UOS thereupon brought an appeal before the Rechtbank (District Court) te Alkmaar (Netherlands). That court found, again on the sole basis of Netherlands law, that the Kantonrechter had erred in finding that it had jurisdiction to hear Mr Weber's case. The Rechtbank te Alkmaar ruled, in substance, that no account could be taken of Mr Weber's employment before 1 February 1993, the date on which the WAMN entered into force, and that the three months he spent working in Danish territorial waters should be given more weight than the time he spent working in the Netherlands continental shelf area.

25. On 7 January 1998 Mr Weber appealed against that decision before the Hoge Raad der Nederlanden, which ruled that the Rechtbank te Alkmaar had erred in law in failing to consider of its own motion whether the rules of the Brussels Convention conferred jurisdiction on the Netherlands courts. In this connection, the Hoge Raad raises two questions: whether, for the purposes of applying Article 5(1) of the Brussels Convention, the work done by Mr Weber in the Netherlands continental shelf area is to be regarded as having been carried out in the Netherlands (and, thus, within the territory of a Contracting State) and whether Mr Weber had, since taking up employment with UOS in July 1987, 'habitually' worked in the Netherlands, within the meaning of Article 5(1).

26. Taking the view that, in the circumstances, resolution of the dispute called for interpretation of the Brussels Convention, the Hoge Raad der Nederlanden decided to stay proceedings and refer the following questions to the Court of Justice for a preliminary ruling:

'1. Must work carried out on the Netherlands section of the continental shelf under the North Sea by an employee as defined in the WAMN be regarded as or treated as equivalent to work carried out in the Netherlands for the purposes of the application of Article 5(1) of the Brussels Convention?

2. If so, in order to answer the question whether the employee must be

regarded as having carried out his work habitually in the Netherlands, must account be taken of the entire period of his employment or is only his most recent period of employment relevant?

3. In answering Question 2 must a distinction be drawn between the period before the WAMN entered into force - when Netherlands law had not yet designated a court with territorial jurisdiction to deal with a case such as the present - and the period after the WAMN entered into force?'

The first question

27. In order to answer the first question it must first be remembered that, according to settled case-law, Article 5(1) of the Brussels Convention is not applicable to contracts of employment performed entirely outside the territory of the Contracting States, since the employee carries out all his work in non-contracting countries (Case 32/88 *Six Constructions* [1989] ECR 341, paragraph 22).

28. Article 5(1) applies only where the individual contract of employment under which the employee carries out his work has a connection with the territory of at least one Contracting State.

29. Secondly, Article 29 of the Vienna Convention on the Law of Treaties of 23 May 1969 states that 'unless a different intention appears from the treaty or is otherwise established, a treaty is binding on each party in respect of its entire territory'.

30. Those are the factors that determine whether or not work carried out in the Netherlands continental shelf area, such as the work in point in the main proceedings, is, for the purposes of applying Article 5(1) of the Brussels Convention, to be regarded as being carried out in the territory of the Netherlands, and thus in the territory of a Contracting State.

31. In the absence of any provision in the Brussels Convention governing that aspect of its scope or any other indication as to the answer to be given to this question, reference must be made to the principles of public international law relating to the legal regime applicable to the continental shelf and, in particular, the Geneva Convention, which applied to the Netherlands at the material time.

32. Under Article 2 of the Geneva Convention, the coastal State exercises over the continental shelf sovereign rights for the purposes of

exploring it and exploiting its natural resources. Those rights are exclusive and do not depend on any express proclamation.

33. Under Article 5 of the same convention, 'the coastal State is entitled to construct and maintain or operate on the continental shelf installations and other devices necessary for its exploration and the exploitation of its natural resources'. Article 5 further provides that those installations and devices are 'under the jurisdiction of the coastal State'.

34. Furthermore, the International Court of Justice has ruled that the rights of the coastal State in respect of the area of continental shelf constituting a natural prolongation of its land territory under the sea exist *ipso facto* and *ab initio* by virtue of the State's sovereignty over the land and by extension of that sovereignty in the form of the exercise of sovereign rights for the purposes of the exploration of the seabed and the exploitation of its natural resources (judgment of 20 February 1969 in the so-called *North Sea Continental Shelf* cases, Reports, 1969, p. 3, paragraph 19).

35. Moreover, it is in conformity with those principles of public international law that Article 10(1) of the WAMN provides that the courts of the Netherlands have jurisdiction in disputes concerning the contracts of employment of employees who work on or from mining installations positioned on or above the Netherlands continental shelf area for the purposes of prospecting and/or exploiting its natural resources.

36. It follows that the answer to the first question must be that work carried out by an employee on fixed or floating installations positioned on or above the part of the continental shelf adjacent to a Contracting State, in the context of the prospecting and/or exploitation of its natural resources, is to be regarded as work carried out in the territory of that State for the purposes of applying Article 5(1) of the Brussels Convention.

The second question

37. In order to answer the second question it is necessary to recall, at the outset, the case-law of the Court of Justice on the interpretation of Article 5(1) of the Brussels Convention where the dispute concerns an individual contract of employment.

38. First of all, it is clear from that case-law that, as regards this type of contract, the place of performance of the obligation upon which the claim

is based, as referred to in Article 5(1) of the Brussels Convention, must be determined not by reference to the applicable national law in accordance with the conflict rules of the court before which the matter is brought, as is the case for most other contracts (settled case-law since Case 12/76 *Tessili* [1976] ECR 1473), but by reference to uniform criteria which it is for the Court to lay down on the basis of the scheme and objectives of the Brussels Convention (see, *inter alia*, Case C-125/92 *Mulox IBC* [1993] ECR I-4075, paragraphs 10, 11 and 16, Case C-383/95 *Rutten* [1997] ECR I-57, paragraphs 12 and 13, and Case C-440/97 *GIE Groupe Concorde and Others* [1999] ECR I-6307, paragraph 14).

39. Secondly, the Court takes the view that the rule on special jurisdiction in Article 5(1) of the Brussels Convention is justified by the existence of a particularly close relationship between a dispute and the court best placed, in order to ensure the proper administration of justice and effective organisation of the proceedings, to take cognisance of the matter, and that the courts for the place in which the employee is to carry out the agreed work are best suited to resolving disputes to which the contractof employment might give rise (see, *inter alia*, *Mulox IBC*, cited above, paragraph 17, and *Rutten*, cited above, paragraph 16).

40. Thirdly, in matters relating to contracts of employment, interpretation of Article 5(1) of the Brussels Convention must take account of the concern to afford proper protection to the employee as the weaker of the contracting parties from the social point of view. Such protection is best assured if disputes relating to a contract of employment fall within the jurisdiction of the courts of the place where the employee discharges his obligations towards his employer, since that is the place where it is least expensive for the employee to commence or defend court proceedings (see, *inter alia*, *Mulox IBC*, paragraphs 18 and 19, and *Rutten*, paragraph 17).

41. It follows that Article 5(1) of the Brussels Convention must be interpreted as meaning that, as regards contracts of employment, the place of performance of the relevant obligation, for the purposes of that provision, is the place where the employee actually performs the work covered by the contract with his employer (*Mulox IBC*, paragraph 20, *Rutten*, paragraph 15, and *GIE Groupe Concorde*, paragraph 14).

42. The Court has also held that, where work is performed in more than one Contracting State, it is important to avoid any multiplication of courts having jurisdiction in order to preclude the risk of irreconcilable deci-

sions and to facilitate the recognition and enforcement of judgments in States other than those in which they were delivered and that, consequently, Article 5(1) of the Brussels Convention cannot be interpreted as conferring concurrent jurisdiction on the courts of each Contracting State in whose territory the employee performs part of his work (*Mulox IBC*, paragraphs 21 and 23, and *Rutten*, paragraph 18).

43. As a result, the Court held, at paragraphs 25 and 26 of its judgment in *Mulox IBC*, that, in such a case, the place of performance of the obligation characterising the contract of employment, within the meaning of Article 5(1) of the Brussels Convention, is the place where or from which the employee principally discharges his obligations towards his employer. It further held that it was necessary to take into account the fact that the work entrusted to the employee was carried out from an office in a Contracting State, where the employee in question had established his residence, from which he worked for his employer and to which he returned after each business trip to another country.

44. In *Rutten* the Court held, in similar circumstances, that the place where an employee habitually carries out his work, within the meaning of Article 5(1) of the Brussels Convention, is the place where he has established the effective centre of his working activities and that, when identifying that place, it is necessary to take into account the fact that the employee spends most of his working time in one of the Contracting States in which he has an office where he organises his work for his employer and to which he returns after each business trip abroad.

45. As regards identifying the place where an employee habitually works, as referred to in Article 5(1), it is appropriate, in a case such as that in the main proceedings, to remember that the factual background of the dispute between Mr Weber and his employer has not yet been fully and clearly established before the national courts.

46. Thus, whilst it is common ground that, from 21 September to 30 December 1993, Mr Weber worked as a cook on board a floating crane in Danish territorial waters, as to the rest, the case-file shows only that he was employed by UOS in the Netherlands continental shelf area on mining vessels or installations within the meaning of the WAMN for at least part of the period from July 1987 to 21 September 1993. In particular, the parties to the main proceedings disagree as to the exact dates within that period on which Mr Weber worked in the area. Nor does the case-file

reveal whether, during that same period, Mr Weber worked for UOS in another place or, if he did, the country or countries concerned and the duration of his work there. The observations of the Rechtbank te Alkmaar indicate only that between 1 February and 21 September 1993 Mr Weber spent 79 days working in the Netherlands continental shelf area, without clearly establishing whether, during the remaining 144 days, he worked elsewhere or took leave.

47. Despite that uncertainty, it is common ground that, during his period of employment with UOS, Mr Weber was engaged in at least two different Contracting States.

48. Furthermore, unlike the employees in *Mulox IBC* and *Rutten*, Mr Weber did not have an office in a Contracting State that constituted the effective centre of his working activities or from which he performed the essential part of his duties *vis-à-vis* his employer.

49. The Court's case-law cannot, therefore, be applied in its entirety to the present case. Nevertheless, it remains relevant to the extent that it means that, where a contract of employment is performed in several Contracting States, Article 5(1) of the Brussels Convention must - in view of the need to establish the place with which the dispute has the most significant link, so that it is possible to identify the courts best placed to decide the case in order to afford proper protection to the employee as the weaker party to the contract and to avoid multiplication of the courts having jurisdiction - be understood as referring to the place where or from which the employee actually performs the essential part of his duties *vis-à-vis* his employer. That is the place where it is least expensive for the employee to commence proceedings against his employer or to defend such proceedings and where the courts best suited to resolving disputes relating to the contract of employment are situated (see *Rutten*, paragraphs 22 to 24).

50. That being so, in a case such as that in the main proceedings, the relevant criterion for establishing an employee's habitual place of work, for the purposes of Article 5(1) of the Brussels Convention, is, in principle, the place where he spends most of his working time engaged on his employer's business.

51. In a case such as that in the main proceedings, in which the employee continuously performed the same job for his employer, namely that of cook, throughout the entire period of employment in question, any qual-

itative criteria relating to the nature and importance of work done in various places within the Contracting States are irrelevant.

52. The logical implication of the temporal criterion mentioned in paragraph 50 of the present judgment, which is based on the relative duration of periods of time spent working in the various Contracting States in question, is that all of an employee's term of employment must be taken into account in establishing the place where he carries out the most significant part of his work and where, in such a case, his contractual relationship with his employer is centred.

53. It would only be if, taking account of the facts of the present case, the subject-matter of the dispute were more closely connected with a different place of work that the principle set out in the preceding paragraph would fail to apply.

54. For example, weight will be given to the most recent period of work where the employee, after having worked for a certain time in one place, then takes up his work activities on a permanent basis in a different place, since the clear intention of the parties is for the latter place to become a new habitual place of work within the meaning of Article 5(1) of the Brussels Convention.

55. On the other hand, in the event that the criteria mentioned in paragraphs 50 to 54 of the present judgment do not enable the national courts to establish the habitual place of work for the purposes of applying Article 5(1) of the Brussels Convention, either because there are two or more places of work of equal importance or because none of the various places where the employee carries on his work activity has a sufficiently permanent and close connection with the work done to be regarded as the main link for the purposes of determining the courts with jurisdiction, it is necessary, as is clear from paragraphs 42 and 49 of the present judgment, to avoid a multiplication of the courts having jurisdiction over a single legal relationship. Article 5(1) of the Brussels Convention cannot, therefore, be interpreted as conferring concurrent jurisdiction on the courts of each Contracting State in whose territory the employee carries on some of his work.

56. In this connection it must be borne in mind that, as is clear from the report of Mr Jenard on the Brussels Convention (OJ 1979 C 59, p. 1, at p. 22), the rules on special jurisdiction merely give the applicant an additional option without, however, affecting the general principle set out in

the first paragraph of Article 2 of the convention that persons domiciled in the territory of a Contracting State may be sued in the courts of that State regardless of the nationality of the parties. Furthermore, the last part of Article 5(1) of the convention provides that, if the employee does not habitually carry out his work in any one country, the employer may 'also' be sued in the courts for the place where the business which engaged the employee was or is now situated.

57. Consequently, in the situation mentioned in paragraph 55 of the present judgment, an employee will have the choice of bringing his action against his employer either before the courts for the place where the business which engaged him is situated, in accordance with the last part of Article 5(1) of the Brussels Convention, or before the courts of the Contracting State on whose territory the employer is domiciled, in accordance with the first paragraph of Article 2 of the convention, assuming those two forums are not one and the same.

58. In light of all of the foregoing considerations, the answer to the second question must be that Article 5(1) of the Brussels Convention must be interpreted as meaning that where an employee performs the obligations arising under his contract of employment in several Contracting States the place where he habitually works, within the meaning of that provision, is the place where, or from which, taking into account all the circumstances of the case, he in fact performs the essential part of his duties *vis-à-vis* his employer.

In the case of a contract of employment under which an employee performs for his employer the same activities in more than one Contracting State, it is necessary, in principle, to take into account the whole of the duration of the employment relationship in order to identify the place where the employee habitually works, within the meaning of Article 5(1).

Failing other criteria, that will be the place where the employee has worked the longest.

It will only be otherwise if, in light of the facts of the case, the subject-matter of the dispute is more closely connected with a different place of work, which would, in that case, be the relevant place for the purposes of applying Article 5(1) of the Brussels Convention.

In the event that the criteria laid down by the Court of Justice do not enable the national court to identify the habitual place of work, as referred to in Article 5(1) of the Brussels Convention, the employee will have the choice of suing his employer either in the courts for the place where the business which engaged him is situated, or in the courts of the Contracting State in whose territory the employer is domiciled.

The third question

59. For this question, it is appropriate first to observe that the object of the Brussels Convention is to determine the jurisdiction of the courts of the Contracting States in the intra-Community legal order in civil and commercial matters with the result that national procedural laws are set aside in matters governed by the convention in favour of the provisions thereof (see Case 25/79 *Sanicentral* [1979] ECR 3423, paragraph 5).

60. Next, it is appropriate to recall that it is settled case-law that the terms used in Article 5(1) of the Brussels Convention must, in matters relating to employment contracts, be interpreted autonomously so as to ensure the full effectiveness and uniform application in all the Contracting States of this convention, whose objectives include unification of the rules on jurisdiction of the Contracting States (see, *inter alia*, *Mulox IBC*, cited above, paragraphs 10 and 16, and *Rutten*, cited above, paragraphs 12 and 13).

61. It follows that national law has no bearing on the application of Article 5(1) of the Brussels Convention and so the date of entry into force of the WAMN has no bearing upon the effect of the provision.

62. That being so, the answer to the third question must be that national law applicable to the main dispute has no bearing on the interpretation of the concept of the place where an employee habitually works, within the meaning of Article 5(1) of the convention, to which the second question relates.

On those grounds,

THE COURT (Sixth Chamber),

in answer to the questions referred to it by the Hoge Raad der Nederlanden by judgment of 4 February 2000, hereby rules:

1. Work carried out by an employee on fixed or floating installa-

tions positioned on or above the part of the continental shelf adjacent to a Contracting State, in the context of the prospecting and/or exploitation of its natural resources, is to be regarded as work carried out in the territory of that State for the purposes of applying Article 5(1) of the Convention of 27 September 1968 on Jurisdiction and the Enforcement of Judgments in Civil and Commercial Matters, as amended by the Convention of 9 October 1978 on the Accession of the Kingdom of Denmark, Ireland and the United Kingdom of Great Britain and Northern Ireland, the Convention of 25 October 1982 on the Accession of the Hellenic Republic and the Convention of 26 May 1989 on the Accession of the Kingdom of Spain and the Portuguese Republic.

2. Article 5(1) of that convention must be interpreted as meaning that where an employee performs the obligations arising under his contract of employment in several Contracting States the place where he habitually works, within the meaning of that provision, is the place where, or from which, taking account of all the circumstances of the case, he in fact performs the essential part of his duties *vis-à-vis* his employer.

In the case of a contract of employment under which an employee performs for his employer the same activities in more than one Contracting State, it is necessary, in principle, to take account of the whole of the duration of the employment relationship in order to identify the place where the employee habitually works, within the meaning of Article 5(1).

Failing other criteria, that will be the place where the employee has worked the longest.

It will only be otherwise if, in light of the facts of the case, the subject-matter of the dispute is more closely connected with a different place of work, which would, in that case, be the relevant place for the purposes of applying Article 5(1) of the convention.

In the event that the criteria laid down by the Court of Justice do not enable the national court to identify the habitual place of work, as referred to in Article 5(1) of the convention, the employee will have the choice of suing his employer either in the courts for the place where the business which engaged him is situated, or in the courts of the Contracting State in whose territory the employer is domiciled.

3. National law applicable to the main dispute has no bearing on the interpretation of the concept of the place where an employee habitually works, within the meaning of Article 5(1) of the convention, to which the second question relates.

Case C-80/00 - 6 June 2002

Italian Leather SpA
v
WECO Polstermöbel GmbH & Co.

Article 27(3) - Irreconcilability - Enforcement procedures in the State where enforcement is sought

JUDGMENT OF THE COURT (Fifth Chamber),

Jann, President of the Chamber, Edward, La Pergola, Wathelet (Rapporteur) andTimmermans, Judges

1. By order of 10 February 2000, received at the Court on 7 March 2000, the Bundesgerichtshof (Federal Court of Justice) referred to the Court for a preliminary ruling under the Protocol of 3 June 1971 on the interpretation by the Court of Justice of the Convention of 27 September 1968 on Jurisdiction and the Enforcement of Judgments in Civil and Commercial Matters three questions on the interpretation of Title III, headed 'Recognition and enforcement', of that Convention (OJ 1978 L 304, p. 36), as amended by the Convention of 9 October 1978 on the Accession of the Kingdom of Denmark, Ireland and the United Kingdom of Great Britain and Northern Ireland (OJ 1978 L 304, p. 1 and - amended text - p. 77), by the Convention of 25 October 1982 on the Accession of the Hellenic Republic (OJ 1982 L 388, p. 1) and by the Convention of 26 May 1989 on the Accession of the Kingdom of Spain and the Portuguese Republic (OJ 1989 L 285, p. 1) (hereinafter 'the Brussels Convention').

2. Those questions were raised in proceedings between Italian Leather SpA (hereinafter 'Italian Leather'), a company governed by Italian law established in Bironto (Italy), and WECO Polstermöbel GmbH & Co. (hereinafter 'WECO'), a limited partnership governed by German law

established in Leimbach (Germany), concerning the conditions of use of a brand name under a contract for the exclusive distribution of leather-upholstered furniture.

Legal context

The Brussels Convention

3. As stated in the first paragraph of Article 1, the Brussels Convention applies in civil and commercial matters whatever the nature of the court or tribunal.

4. Article 24 of the Brussels Convention states:

'Application may be made to the courts of a Contracting State for such provisional, including protective, measures as may be available under the law of that State, even if, under this Convention, the courts of another Contracting State have jurisdiction as to the substance of the matter.'

5. Title III of the Brussels Convention lays down the rules under which judgments given by the courts of a Contracting State are recognised and enforced in the other Contracting States.

6. Article 25 of the Brussels Convention provides:

'For the purposes of this Convention, judgment means any judgment given by a court or tribunal of a Contracting State, whatever the judgment may be called, including a decree, order, decision or writ of execution, as well as the determination of costs or expenses by an officer of the court.'

7. The first paragraph of Article 26 of the Brussels Convention states:

'A judgment given in a Contracting State shall be recognised in the other Contracting States without any special procedure being required.'

8. Article 27 of the Brussels Convention is worded as follows:

'A judgment shall not be recognised:

...

3. if the judgment is irreconcilable with a judgment given in a dispute between the same parties in the State in which recognition is sought;

...'

9. The first paragraph of Article 31 of the Brussels Convention states:

'A judgment given in a Contracting State and enforceable in that State shall be enforced in another Contracting State when, on the application of any interested party, it has been declared enforceable there.'

10. The first paragraph of Article 34 of the Brussels Convention provides:

'The court applied to shall give its decision without delay; the party against whom enforcement is sought shall not at this stage of the proceedings be entitled to make any submissions on the application.'

German legislation

11. According to the Bundesgerichtshof, under Paragraph 935 of the Zivilprozessordnung (German Code of Civil Procedure, hereinafter 'the ZPO') an interim measure may be granted if it is feared that a change in the current situation could prevent or substantially impede the assertion by a party of his rights. Accordingly, the court seised is called on essentially to maintain the status quo.

12. The Bundesgerichtshof further points out that, under Paragraph 940 of the ZPO, the court seised may also make an interim order regulating a legal relationship, in so far as that appears to be necessary in order to prevent substantial prejudice or imminent use of force or for other reasons.

13. Under Paragraph 890(1) of the ZPO, decisions of German courts which impose restraining orders may also give rise to an administrative penalty payment or, where such payment cannot be recovered, to imprisonment.

The main proceedings and the questions referred for a preliminary ruling

14. Italian Leather is a company which sells leather-upholstered furniture under the name 'LongLife'. WECO sells furniture of the same type.

15. In 1996 Italian Leather granted WECO, under an 'exclusive contract', the right to distribute its goods for five years within a specified geographical area. That contract contained *inter alia* the following clauses:

'(2) Dealers may use the LongLife brand name only when marketing suites that are covered in LongLife leather.

...

(4) No dealer may use the LongLife brand name for its own advertising without written authorisation from the supplier.'

16. The parties agreed that the courts of Bari (Italy) would have jurisdiction to deal with disputes relating to that contract.

17. In 1998 WECO complained of defective performance of the contract by Italian Leather. It informed Italian Leather that, as a consequence, it would not be a party to any joint sales message at forthcoming exhibitions and that it would present its own WECO mark.

18. Italian Leather brought proceedings for interim relief against WECO before the Landgericht Koblenz (Regional Court, Koblenz, Germany), the court within whose jurisdiction WECO's registered office is situated, to restrain it from marketing products presented as being in easy-care leather under the brand name 'naturia longlife by Maurizio Danieli'.

19. By judgment of 17 November 1998 the Landgericht Koblenz, which had been seised in accordance with Article 24 of the Brussels Convention, dismissed the application because there was no 'ground justifying the grant of interim relief'.

20. The Landgericht Koblenz took the view that to grant Italian Leather's application would be tantamount to ordering WECO to perform the contract. However, Italian Leather had not proved that there was a risk of irreparable damage or of a definitive loss of rights, conditions which had to be met under German law before the relief sought could be granted. Furthermore, WECO had already taken concrete steps to advertise and market its products with leather from other suppliers. Accordingly, it too would suffer considerable damage if the prohibition sought were granted.

21. A few days before the Landgericht Koblenz delivered its judgment of 17 November 1998, Italian Leather had applied to the Tribunale di Bari (Bari District Court) for interim measures. In its order of 28 December 1998, the Tribunale di Bari took a different view on the condition of urgency. It held in this regard that 'the *periculum in mora* (urgency) lies in the plaintiff's economic loss and the possible extinction of its rights resulting therefrom, for which there would be no compensation'.

22. Consequently, the Tribunale di Bari prohibited WECO from using the word 'LongLife' for the distribution of its leather furniture products in certain Member States, including Germany.

23. On application by Italian Leather, the Landgericht Koblenz, by order of 18 January 1999 (hereinafter 'the order for enforcement'), endorsed a warrant for execution in the order of the Tribunale di Bari, coupling it with a financial penalty on the basis of Paragraph 890(1) of the ZPO.

24. On an appeal brought by WECO, the Oberlandesgericht (the competent Higher Regional Court) varied the order for enforcement, holding that the order of the Tribunale di Bari was irreconcilable, within the meaning of Article 27(3) of the Brussels Convention, with the judgment of 17 November 1998 by which the Landgericht Koblenz had dismissed Italian Leather's application seeking to prohibit WECO from using the LongLife brand name for the marketing of its leather products.

25. Italian Leather appealed against the decision of the Oberlandesgericht to the Bundesgerichtshof.

26. The Bundesgerichtshof is unsure as to the correct interpretation of Article 27(3) of the Brussels Convention.

27. According to the Bundesgerichtshof, the Court of Justice's case-law on whether the legal consequences of different judgments are mutually exclusive has, until now, only concerned situations in which there were divergences in substantive law. However, the case before the Bundesgerichtshof has the particular feature that the conflict between the two decisions on interim measures at issue is attributable only to divergences as to procedural requirements.

28. The Bundesgerichtshof states that, if those decisions are irreconcilable, the court of the State in which enforcement is sought should nevertheless have the power to disapply Article 27(3) of the Brussels Convention if it considers that, from the point of view of that State, the divergence is not sufficiently significant. The sole purpose of Article 27(3) is to prevent the rule of law in a Contracting State from being disrupted by advantage being taken of two conflicting judgments. The risk of such disruption in a given case is to be assessed solely from the point of view of the State in which enforcement is sought.

29. The Bundesgerichtshof is also uncertain whether, if it were to uphold the order for enforcement, it may, or must, maintain the financial penalty which the Landgericht Koblenz, on the basis of German law, attached to the order of the Tribunale di Bari in case the latter order was not enforced.

30. Pointing out that the Brussels Convention is designed to further the transnational recognition of judgments, the Bundesgerichtshof interprets the first paragraph of Article 31 and the first paragraph of Article 34 of the Convention as, in general terms, requiring the court of the State where enforcement of a foreign judicial decision is sought to create, so far as possible, the same favourable conditions for its enforcement as apply to a comparable decision of a national court.

31. In this connection, the Bundesgerichtshof observes that under Italian law there is no direct method of enforcement of restraining orders other than payment of damages.

32. Accordingly, the application of coercive measures provided for by German law in order to enforce immediately a restraining order made by an Italian court would have more powerful effects than those envisaged by the law of the State of origin. The Bundesgerichtshof has doubts as to whether the first paragraph of Article 31 and the first paragraph of Article 34 of the Brussels Convention permit or require such a solution.

33. Consequently, the Bundesgerichtshof decided to stay proceedings and refer the following questions to the Court for a preliminary ruling:

'(1) Can judgments be irreconcilable within the meaning of Article 27(3) of the Brussels Convention when the only difference between them lies in the specific requirements for the adoption of a particular type of autonomous provisional measure (within the meaning of Article 24 of the Convention)?

(2) May and must the court of the State of enforcement which has declared a foreign judgment requiring the party against whom enforcement is sought to desist from certain activities to be enforceable in accordance with the firstparagraph of Article 34 and the first paragraph of Article 31 of the Convention at the same time order the measures necessary, under the law of the State of enforcement, for enforcement of a restraining order?

(3) If the answer to Question 2 is in the affirmative, must the measures

necessary, under the law of the State of enforcement, for enforcement of the restraining order be ordered even if the judgment to be recognised does not itself include comparable measures in accordance with the law of the State of origin, and that law makes no provision at all for the immediate enforceability of such restraining orders?'

Question 1

34. By this question, the national court is essentially asking, first, whether, on a proper construction of Article 27(3) of the Brussels Convention, a foreign decision on interim measures ordering an obligor not to carry out certain acts is irreconcilable with a decision on interim measures refusing to grant such an order in a dispute between the same parties in the State where recognition is sought, even though the respective effects of those decisions are attributable to divergences as to the procedural requirements for the grant of such an order under the national law of the State of origin and of the State where recognition is sought. If so, it asks, second, whether a court of the latter State is required to refuse to recognise the foreign decision or whether the Brussels Convention allows it to refuse recognition only if it finds that the coexistence of two conflicting decisions would cause real and appreciable disruption to the rule of law in the State where recognition is sought.

Observations of the parties

35. So far as concerns the first part of the first question, the United Kingdom Government submits in its written observations that the concept of irreconcilability requires the court of the State in which recognition is sought to draw certain distinctions, such as that existing between the procedural requirements for the adoption of a particular type of measure and the effects of the judgment adopting or refusing to grant such a measure, or the distinction between the substantive and procedural requirements upon which grant of the measure sought is conditional.

36. The United Kingdom Government observes with regard to the first distinction that Article 27(3) of the Brussels Convention concerns solely the legal effects of a judgment and not the procedural requirements for its adoption. Examination of those requirements may, however, be necessary in order to determine the legal effects of the judgment concerned and to assess, by way of consequence, to what extent it is irreconcilable with another judgment. That is particularly the case where the measure sought has been refused. It may then be necessary to refer to the requirements for the adoption of the measure in order to understand the content of the judgment refusing to grant it.

37. As regards the second distinction referred to in paragraph 35 of the present judgment, the court may, in order to appraise the content and effect of each of the competing judgments, examine whether the requirements for the adoption of the measures in question are substantive or procedural. That will be particularly true where the court of the State in which recognition is sought is faced with a judgment refusing to order a particular measure because, in that case, there will be no 'measure' as such to examine.

38. At the hearing, the United Kingdom Government inferred therefrom that, in the main proceedings, it was difficult to regard the negative effects of the judgment of 17 November 1998 of the Landgericht Koblenz as being irreconcilable with the positive effects of the order of the Tribunale di Bari of 28 December 1998. Only if the respective criteria applied by those two courts and the evidence adduced before them were identical could the effects of the decisions made by them be regarded as irreconcilable.

Findings of the Court

39. By way of preliminary point, the Court proceeds on the assumption that, the court competent to adjudicate on the substance being the Tribunale di Bari, the Landgericht Koblenz did not by its judgment of 17 November 1998 exceed the limits, as interpreted by the Court, of the jurisdiction which it derived from Article 24 of the Brussels Convention (see Case C-391/95 *Van Uden* [1998] ECR I-7091, paragraphs 37 to 47, and Case C-99/96 *Mietz* [1999] ECR I-2277, paragraphs 42, 46 and 47).

40. First, it is clear from the Court's case-law that, in order to ascertain whether two judgments are irreconcilable within the meaning of Article 27(3) of the Brussels Convention, it should be examined whether they entail legal consequences that are mutually exclusive (Case 145/86 *Hoffmann* [1988] ECR 645, paragraph 22).

41. Second, it is unimportant whether the judgments at issue have been delivered in proceedings for interim measures or in proceedings on the substance. As Article 27(3) of the Brussels Convention, following the example of Article 25, refers to 'judgments' without further precision, it has general application. Consequently, decisions on interim measures are subject to the rules laid down by the Convention concerning irreconcilability in the same way as the other 'judgments' covered by Article 25.

42. Third, it is equally immaterial that national procedural rules as to interim measures are liable to vary from one Contracting State to another to a greater degree than rules governing proceedings on the substance.

43. The object of the Brussels Convention is not to unify the procedural rules of the Contracting States, but to determine which court has jurisdiction in disputes concerning civil and commercial matters in intra-Community relations and to facilitate the enforcement of judgments (see Case C-365/88 *Hagen* [1990] ECR I-1845, paragraph 17, and Case C-68/93 *Shevill and Others* [1995] ECR I-415, paragraph 35).

44. Moreover, as follows from paragraph 22 of the judgment in *Hoffmann*, cited above, irreconcilability lies in the effects of judgments. It does not concern the requirements governing admissibility and procedure which determine whether judgment can be given and which may vary from one Contracting State to another.

45. In the light of the foregoing, it is clear that decisions on interim measures such as the decisions here at issue in the main proceedings are irreconcilable.

46. The Tribunale di Bari granted the application made by Italian Leather seeking to prohibit WECO from using the LongLife brand name for the marketing of its leather products after the Landgericht Koblenz had dismissed an identical application made by the same plaintiff against the same defendant.

47. The answer to the first part of the first question must therefore be that, on a proper construction of Article 27(3) of the Brussels Convention, a foreign decision on interim measures ordering an obligor not to carry out certain acts is irreconcilable with a decision on interim measures refusing to grant such an order in a dispute between the same parties in the State where recognition is sought.

48. As regards the second part of the first question, concerning the consequences which result where a foreign judgment and a judgment of a court of the State in which recognition is sought are irreconcilable, it should be noted first of all that, as stated in the Jenard Report on the Brussels Convention (OJ 1979 C 59, p. 1, at p. 45), 'there can be no doubt that the rule of law in a State would be disturbed if it were possible to take advantage of two conflicting judgments'.

49. Next, it must be remembered that Article 27(3) of the Brussels Convention provides that a judgment is not to be recognised if it is irreconcilable with a judgment given in a dispute between the same parties in the State in which recognition is sought.

50. Article 27(3) of the Brussels Convention therefore sets out a ground for refusing to recognise judgments which is mandatory, in contrast to the second paragraph of Article 28 of the Convention on Jurisdiction and the Enforcement of Judgments in Civil and Commercial Matters, done at Lugano on 16 September 1988 (OJ 1988 L 319, p. 9), under which recognition of a judgment may be refused in any case provided for in Articles 54B(3) or 57(4) of that Convention.

51. Finally, it would be contrary to the principle of legal certainty, which the Court has repeatedly held to be one of the objectives of the Brussels Convention (see Case 38/81 *Effer* [1982] ECR 825, paragraph 6, Case C-440/97 *GIE Groupe Concorde and Others*[1999] ECR I-6307, paragraph 23, and Case C-256/00 *Besix* [2002] ECR I-0000, paragraph 24), to interpret Article 27(3) as conferring on the court of the State in which recognition is sought the power to authorise recognition of a foreign judgment when it is irreconcilable with a judgment given in that Contracting State.

52. In view of the foregoing, the answer to the second part of the first question must be that, where a court of the State in which recognition is sought finds that a judgment of a court of another Contracting State is irreconcilable with a judgment given by a court of the former State in a dispute between the same parties, it is required to refuse to recognise the foreign judgment.

Questions 2 and 3

53. In view of the answer given to the first question, there is no need to answer the second and third questions.

On those grounds,

THE COURT (Fifth Chamber),

in answer to the questions referred to it by the Bundesgerichtshof by order of 10 February 2000, hereby rules:

1. On a proper construction of Article 27(3) of the Convention of 27 September 1968 on Jurisdiction and the Enforcement of Judgments in Civil and Commercial Matters, as amended by the

Convention of 9 October 1978 on the Accession of the Kingdom of Denmark, Ireland and the United Kingdom of Great Britain and Northern Ireland, by the Convention of 25 October 1982 on the Accession of the Hellenic Republic and by the Convention of 26 May 1989 on the Accession of the Kingdom of Spain and the Portuguese Republic, a foreign decision on interim measures ordering an obligor not to carry out certain acts is irreconcilable with a decision on interim measures refusing to grant such an order in a dispute between the same parties in the State where recognition is sought.

2. Where a court of the State in which recognition is sought finds that a judgment of a court of another Contracting State is irreconcilable with a judgment given by a court of the former State in a dispute between the same parties, it is required to refuse to recognise the foreign judgment.

Case C-96/00 - 11 July 2002

Rudolf Gabriel

Request for interpretation of Articles 5(1) and (3) and 13, first paragraph, point 3 - Entitlement of a consumer to whom misleading advertising has been sent to seek payment, in judicial proceedings, of the prize which he has apparently won - Classification - Action of a contractual nature covered by Article 13, first paragraph, point 3 - Conditions

JUDGMENT OF THE COURT (Sixth Chamber),

Macken, President of the Chamber, Gulmann, Schintgen (Rapporteur), Skouris and Cunha Rodrigues, Judges

1. By order of 15 February 2000, received at the Court on 13 March 2000, the Oberster Gerichtshof (Supreme Court, Austria) referred to the Court for a preliminary ruling, pursuant to the Protocol of 3 June 1971 on the interpretation by the Court of Justice of the Convention of 27 September 1968 on Jurisdiction and the Enforcement of Judgments in Civil and Commercial Matters, a question on the interpretation of Articles 5(1) and (3) and 13, first paragraph, point 3, of that Convention (OJ 1978 L 304, p. 36), as amended by the Convention of 9 October 1978 on the Accession of the Kingdom of Denmark, Ireland and the United Kingdom of Great Britain and Northern Ireland (OJ 1978 L 304, p. 1 and - amended text - p. 77), by the Convention of 25 October 1982 on the Accession of the Hellenic Republic (OJ 1982 L 388, p. 1), by the Convention of 26 May 1989 on the Accession of the Kingdom of Spain and the Portuguese Republic (OJ 1989 L 285, p. 1), and by the Convention of 29 November 1996 on the Accession of the Republic of Austria, the Republic of Finland and the Kingdom of Sweden (OJ 1997 C 15, p. 1) ('the Brussels Convention').

2. That question has arisen in proceedings brought before the Oberster Gerichtshof by Mr Gabriel, an Austrian national domiciled in Vienna, for the purpose of determining the court having jurisdiction *ratione loci* to give judgment in the action which he proposes to bring in his State of domicile against a mail-order company established in Germany.

The legal framework

The Brussels Convention

3. The rules on jurisdiction laid down by the Brussels Convention are set out in Title II thereof, which consists of Articles 2 to 24.

4. The first paragraph of Article 2 of the Brussels Convention, which forms part of Section 1, entitled 'General provisions', of Title II, sets out the basic rule in the following terms:

'Subject to the provisions of this Convention, persons domiciled in a Contracting State shall, whatever their nationality, be sued in the courts of that State.'

5. The first paragraph of Article 3 of the Brussels Convention, which features in the same section, provides:

'Persons domiciled in a Contracting State may be sued in the courts of another Contracting State only by virtue of the rules set out in Sections 2 to 6 of this Title.'

6. Articles 5 to 18 of the Brussels Convention, which make up Sections 2 to 6 of Title II thereof, lay down rules governing special, mandatory or exclusive jurisdiction.

7. Thus, under Article 5, which appears in Section 2, entitled 'Special jurisdiction', of Title II of the Brussels Convention:

'A person domiciled in a Contracting State may, in another Contracting State, be sued:

1. in matters relating to a contract, in the courts for the place of performance of the obligation in question; ...

...

3. in matters relating to tort, delict or quasi-delict, in the courts for the place where the harmful event occurred;

...'.

8. Also under Title II of the Brussels Convention, Articles 13 and 14 form part of Section 4, entitled 'Jurisdiction over consumer contracts'.

9. Article 13 of the Brussels Convention is worded as follows:

'In proceedings concerning a contract concluded by a person for a purpose which can be regarded as being outside his trade or profession, hereinafter called the consumer, jurisdiction shall be determined by this Section, without prejudice to the provisions of point 5 of Articles 4 and 5, if it is:

1. a contract for the sale of goods on instalment credit terms; or

2. a contract for a loan repayable by instalments, or for any other form of credit, made to finance the sale of goods; or

3. any other contract for the supply of goods or a contract for the supply of services, and

(a) in the State of the consumer's domicile the conclusion of the contract was preceded by a specific invitation addressed to him or by advertising; and

(b) the consumer took in that State the steps necessary for the conclusion of the contract.

Where a consumer enters into a contract with a party who is not domiciled in a Contracting State but has a branch, agency or other establishment in one of the Contracting States, that party shall, in disputes arising out of the operations of the branch, agency or establishment, be deemed to be domiciled in that State.

This Section shall not apply to contracts of transport.'

10. The first paragraph of Article 14 of the Brussels Convention provides:

'A consumer may bring proceedings against the other party to a contract either in the courts of the Contracting State in which that party is domiciled or in the courts of the Contracting State in which he is himself domiciled.'

11. That rule of jurisdiction may be departed from only if there is compliance with the conditions laid down in Article 15 of the Brussels Convention, which also features in Section 4 of Title II thereof.

The relevant provisions of national law

12. Under Paragraph 28.1.1 of the Austrian Law of 1 August 1895 on the exercise of jurisdiction and the competence of the ordinary courts in civil matters (Jurisdiktionsnorm (Law on Jurisdiction), RGBl. 111), the Oberster Gerichtshof must, when so requested by a party, designate, from among the courts having jurisdiction *ratione materiae* to deal with a civil matter, the court which will be territorially competent where the Austrian court having local jurisdiction is not designated by the rules laid down in that Law or by any other legal provision, but jurisdiction must none the less be exercised pursuant to an international convention.
13. It is common ground that the Brussels Convention is an international convention within the meaning of that provision.

14. Paragraph 5j of the Austrian Consumer Protection Law (BGBl. I, 1979, p. 140) reads:

'Undertakings which send prize notifications or other similar communications to specific consumers, and by the wording of those communications give the impression that a consumer has won a particular prize, must give that prize to the consumer; it may also be claimed in legal proceedings.'

15. That provision was added to the Consumer Protection Law by Paragraph 4 of the Austrian Law on Distance Contracts (BGBl. I, 1999, p. 185) when Directive 97/7/EC of the European Parliament and of the Council of 20 May 1997 on the protection of consumers in respect of distance contracts (OJ 1997 L 144, p. 19) was transposed into Austrian law.

16. That provision entered into force on 1 October 1999.

17. In its order for reference, the Oberster Gerichtshof points out that the purpose of Paragraph 5j is to grant consumers who have been misled by reason of the fact that a professional contacted them personally, creating within them the impression that they had won a prize, whereas the true nature of the transaction is explained only in small print or in an inconspicuous place in the correspondence and in terms difficult to understand, a right to bring legal proceedings to seek enforcement of such a 'promise of financial benefit'.

The case in the main proceedings and the question submitted for preliminary ruling

18. According to the documents relating to the case in the main pro-

ceedings, Schlank & Schick GmbH ('Schlank & Schick'), a company established under German law and having its registered office in Lindau (Germany), sells goods by mail order in, *inter alia*, Germany, Austria, France, Belgium and Switzerland.

19. In October 1999 Mr Gabriel received at his private address and in a sealed envelope several personalised letters from Schlank & Schick which he claims were of such a kind as to lead him to believe that, following a draw, he was the lucky winner of ATS 49 700 and that he was entitled to receive that amount simply on demand, subject only to the condition that he ordered at the same time from that company goods to a minimum value of ATS 200, to be selected in a catalogue and entered on an order form attached to those letters.

20. Those letters stated *inter alia* as follows: 'Dear Mr Rudolf Gabriel, you have not yet claimed your cash credit. ... Do you really want to forfeit your money? ... You are still entitled to your cash credit, but now you really must act quickly. The attached letter from European Credit explains everything in greater detail ... PS. By way of proof for you, Mr Gabriel, I have attached the payment receipt. You are entitled to 100% of your cash credit on condition that you also order goods without incurring any obligation.'

21. A letter annexed to that mail, headed 'European Credit' and entitled 'Official confirmation of payment', to which were annexed the copy of a 'receipt' and the facsimile of a 'savings book', both of which bore Mr Gabriel's name and the amount of ATS 49 700, was worded as follows: 'Dear Mr Rudolf Gabriel, we hereby confirm to you once again the payment to our account of the cash credit amount totalling ATS 49 700. We have attached specially for you a copy of a receipt. In order to seize your opportunity and speed up payment of the sum of ATS 49 700, all you have to do is return the copy of the receipt together with your test order, which does not involve any obligation ... There is now nothing further to prevent payment. In order that you can receive your money as quickly as possible, I shall simply send you a cheque after the receipt has been received. You will then be able to encash it as you please at the financial institution of your choice.'

22. It appears, however, from various statements printed in relatively small characters and featuring in part on the reverse side of the documents sent to Mr Gabriel that the sum of ATS 49 700 did not constitute a firm promise on the part of Schlank & Schick to pay the prize.

23. Thus, on the reverse of the letter from 'European Credit', it was stated *inter alia*, under the heading 'Award Conditions', that participation in the 'winning game', governed by German law, was subject to the placing of a 'test order, which does not involve any obligation', that the expiry date for this 'action' was 30 November 1999 and that all judicial proceedings were excluded. Reference was also made to the fact that the draw had been made by the mail-order company, that the cash prizes were divided into 'different lots' being the subject of several payments split up according to the number of copies of receipts returned to the organiser with the properly filled-out order form, and that, on grounds of cost, the 'credits' having a value lower than ATS 35 would not result in any payment but would be placed in the jackpot for a later draw.

24. Mr Gabriel duly filled out and returned to Schlank & Schick the relevant documents to claim payment of the financial benefit promised and placed an order for goods in that company's catalogue for an amount in excess of ATS 200.

25. Schlank & Schick subsequently delivered to him the goods which he had ordered but did not send him the sum of ATS 49 700 which he claimed to have won.

26. Mr Gabriel accordingly decided to institute legal proceedings for an order requiring Schlank & Schick to pay him that amount, together with interest and legal costs, pursuant to Paragraph 5j of the Austrian Consumer Protection Law.

27. As he wished to bring that action in Austria - the State in which he is domiciled - pursuant to the first paragraph of Article 14 of the Brussels Convention, but as he considered that Austrian law does not contain any provision determining the national court having territorial jurisdiction to hear and determine the case, Mr Gabriel, before lodging the application containing his substantive claim, referred the matter to the Oberster Gerichtshof in order that it might designate that court pursuant to Paragraph 28.1.1 of the Austrian Law of 1 August 1895.

28. The Oberster Gerichtshof takes the view that, while the action which Mr Gabriel proposes to bring appears to be covered by Paragraph 5j of the Austrian Consumer Protection Law, the question whether his application for designation of the national court having territorial jurisdiction should be granted depends on the nature of the action which Mr Gabriel intends to bring against Schlank & Schick.

29. If that action relates to a contract concluded by a consumer within the meaning of Article 13, first paragraph, point 3, of the Brussels Convention, such a designation will be indispensable because that Convention allows a consumer only to bring the dispute before the courts of the Contracting State in which he is domiciled but does not determine directly which court of that State has jurisdiction to give judgment in that regard.

30. In contrast, the application pending before the Oberster Gerichtshof would serve no purpose if Mr Gabriel's right of action were contractual in nature, within the meaning of Article 5(1) of the Brussels Convention, or relating to tort, delict or quasi-delict within the meaning of Article 5(3) thereof, on the ground that those provisions specifically designate the courts having territorial jurisdiction, that is to say, respectively, the courts for the place of performance of the contractual obligation in question or those for the place where the harmful event occurred.

31. As it formed the view that, in those circumstances, the reply to the request which Mr Gabriel had made to it depended on the interpretation of the Brussels Convention, the Oberster Gerichtshof decided to stay proceedings and to refer the following question to the Court for a preliminary ruling:

'For the purposes of the Brussels Convention ..., does the provision in Paragraph 5j of the Austrian Consumer Protection Law ..., in the version of Art I, para. 2, of the Austrian Law on Distance Contracts ..., which entitles certain consumers to claim from undertakings in the courts prizes ostensibly won by them where the undertakings send (or have sent) them prize notifications or other similar communications worded so as to give the impression that they have won a particular prize, constitute:

(1) a contractual claim under Article 13(3); or

(2) a contractual claim under Article 5(1); or

(3) a claim in respect of a tort, delict or quasi-delict under Article 5(3)?'

The question submitted for preliminary ruling

32. Having regard to the factual background to the case in the main proceedings, the question posed must be construed as asking essentially whether the jurisdiction rules set out in the Brussels Convention are to be interpreted as meaning that judicial proceedings by which a consumer seeks an order, in the Contracting State in which he is domiciled and pursuant to that State's legislation, requiring a mail-order company established in another Contracting State to pay him a financial benefit in cir-

cumstances where that company had sent to that consumer in person a letter likely to create the impression that a prize would be awarded to him on condition that he ordered goods to a specified amount, and where that consumer actually placed such an order in the State of his domicile without, however, obtaining payment of that financial benefit, are contractual in nature in the sense contemplated in Articles 5(1) or 13, first paragraph, point 3, of the Brussels Convention, or relating to tort, delict or quasi-delict within the meaning of Article 5(3) thereof.

33. In order to reply to the question as thus reformulated, it should be noted at the outset that, according to settled case-law, the concept of matters relating to tort, delict or quasi-delict within the meaning of Article 5(3) of the Brussels Convention covers allactions which seek to establish the liability of a defendant and which are not related to a contract within the meaning of Article 5(1) of that Convention (see, *inter alia*, Case 189/87 *Kalfelis* [1988] ECR 5565, paragraph 17; Case C-261/90 *Reichert and Kockler* [1992] ECR I-2149, paragraph 16; and Case C-51/97 *Réunion Européenne and Others* [1998] ECR I-6511, paragraph 22).

34. It is thus necessary in the first instance to examine whether an action such as that in point in the main proceedings is contractual in nature.

35. In that connection, it must be observed that Article 5(1) of the Brussels Convention relates to contractual matters in general, whereas Article 13 thereof specifically covers various types of contracts concluded by consumers.

36. As Article 13 of the Brussels Convention thus constitutes a *lex specialis* in relation to Article 5(1) thereof, it is first of all necessary to determine whether an action having the characteristics set out in the question referred for a preliminary ruling, as reformulated, can fall within the scope of the former of those two provisions.

37. According to settled case-law, the concepts used in Article 13 of the Brussels Convention must be interpreted independently, by reference principally to the system and objectives of the Convention, in order to ensure that it is fully effective (see, in particular, Case 150/77 *Bertrand* [1978] ECR 1431, paragraphs 14, 15 and 16; Case C-89/91 *Shearson Lehman Hutton* [1993] ECR I-139, paragraph 13; Case C-269/95 *Benincasa* [1997] ECR I-3767, paragraph 12; and Case C-99/96 *Mietz* [1999] ECR I-2277, paragraph 26).

38. It follows from the actual wording of Article 13 that it is applicable only in so far as the action relates generally to a contract concluded by a consumer for a purpose outside his trade or profession.

39. It follows from that wording, and from the purpose of the special regime introduced by the provisions of Title II, Section 4, of the Brussels Convention, which is to ensure adequate protection for the consumer as the contracting party deemed to be economically weaker and less experienced in legal matters than his professional co-contractor, that those provisions cover only a private final consumer, not engaged in trade or professional activities, who is bound by one of the three types of contract listed in Article 13 of that Convention and who is also personally a party to the action, in accordance with Article 14 thereof (see *Shearson Lehman Hutton*, cited above, paragraphs 19, 20, 22 and 24).

40. With regard, more specifically, to a contract for the supply of services - other than a contract of transport, which is excluded from the scope of Section 4 of Title II of the Brussels Convention pursuant to the third paragraph of Article 13 thereof - or a contract for the supply of goods, as referred to in Article 13, first paragraph, point 3, that provision sets out two additional conditions of application, namely that the conclusion of the contract was preceded in the State of the consumer's domicile by a specific invitation addressed to him or by advertising, and that the consumer took in that State the steps necessary for the conclusion of that contract.

41. As is clear from the Schlosser Report on the Convention on the Accession of the Kingdom of Denmark, Ireland and the United Kingdom of Great Britain and Northern Ireland to the Brussels Convention (OJ 1979 C 59, p. 71, at p. 118), those two concurrent conditions are designed to ensure that there are close connections between the contract in issue and the State in which the consumer is domiciled.

42. With regard to the scope of the concepts employed in those conditions, Professor Schlosser refers, at page 119 of his report, to the Giuliano and Lagarde Report on the Convention on the law applicable to contractual obligations (OJ 1980 C 282, p. 1), which was opened for signature in Rome on 19 June 1980 (OJ 1980 L 266, p. 1) ('the Rome Convention'), in view of the fact that Article 5(2), first indent, of that Convention, relating to consumer contracts, contains two conditions which use wording identical to that in Article 13, first paragraph, point 3(a) and (b), of the Brussels Convention.

43. According to the Giuliano and Lagarde Report, that provision of the Rome Convention is intended to cover situations in which the trader has taken steps to market his goods or services in the country where the consumer resides and, *inter alia*, situations of mail-order and doorstep selling (see the above Report, pages 23 and 24).

44. The concepts of 'advertising' and 'specific invitation addressed' featuring in the first of those conditions common to the Brussels and Rome Conventions cover all forms of advertising carried out in the Contracting State in which the consumer is domiciled, whether disseminated generally by the press, radio, television, cinema or any other medium, or addressed directly, for example by means of catalogues sent specifically to that State, as well as commercial offers made to the consumer in person, in particular by an agent or door-to-door salesman.

45. With regard to the second of those conditions, the expression 'steps necessary for the conclusion' of the contract refers to any document written or any other step whatever taken by the consumer in the State in which he is domiciled and which expresses his wish to take up the invitation made by the professional.

46. It must be concluded that all of those conditions are satisfied in a case such as that in the main proceedings.

47. First, it is common ground that Mr Gabriel has in this case the capacity of a private final consumer covered by the first paragraph of Article 13 of the Brussels Convention inasmuch as it is clear from the case-file that he ordered goods offered by Schlank & Schick for his personal use, without that transaction having any connection whatever with his trade or profession.

48. Second, in a situation such as that in point in the main proceedings, the consumer and the professional vendor were indubitably linked contractually once Mr Gabriel had ordered goods offered by Schlank & Schick, thereby demonstrating his acceptance of the offer - including all conditions attaching thereto - which that company had sent to him in person.

49. Furthermore, that concordance of intention between the two parties gave rise to reciprocal and interdependent obligations within the framework of a contract which has specifically one of the objects described in Article 13, first paragraph, point 3, of the Brussels Convention.

50. Thus, in regard to a case such as that in the main proceedings, that contract relates more specifically to the supply, through a mail-order sale, of goods ordered by a consumer on the basis of a proposal made and at a price specified by the vendor.

51. Third, the two conditions specifically set out in Article 13, first paragraph, point 3(a) and (b), of the Brussels Convention are also satisfied.

52. The vendor addressed the consumer in the Contracting State in which the latter was domiciled by sending him several personalised letters, to which were attached a sales catalogue and an order form, with a view to persuading him to contract on the basis of those proposals and the conditions relating thereto. Furthermore, as a result of those letters, the consumer took in that State the steps necessary to conclude the contract by placing an order for the amount stipulated by the vendor and by sending to the vendor the order form together with the copy of the 'receipt'.

53. In those circumstances, where a consumer has been contacted at his home by one or more letters sent by a professional vendor for the purpose of bringing about the placement of an order for goods offered under the conditions determined by that vendor, and where the consumer has in fact placed such an order in the Contracting State in which he is domiciled, the action by which such a consumer seeks through judicial proceedings brought against the vendor to obtain a prize which he has apparently won is an action relating to a contract concluded by a consumer within the meaning of Article 13, first paragraph, point 3, of the Brussels Convention.

54. As is evident from the case-file placed before the Court, the right of a consumer to bring an action is intimately linked to the contract concluded between the parties inasmuch as, in a situation such as that in point in the main proceedings, the correspondence which the profession al sent to that consumer establishes an indissociable relationship between the promise of financial benefit and the order for goods, that order being presented by the vendor as constituting the prerequisite for the grant of the promised financial benefit, specifically for the purpose of persuading the consumer to enter into a contract. Furthermore, the consumer concluded the contract for the purchase of goods essentially, if indeed not exclusively, by reason of the vendor's proposal involving a promise of financial benefit significantly greater than theminimum amount required for the order and the consumer otherwise met all of the conditions laid down by the professional, thereby accepting that professional's proposal in its entirety.

55. Consequently, judicial proceedings by which a consumer seeks an order, in the Contracting State in which he is domiciled, requiring a mail-order company established in another Contracting State to send to him a prize which he has apparently won must be capable of being brought before the same court as that which has jurisdiction to deal with the contract concluded by that consumer.

56. An interpretation of Article 13, first paragraph, of the Brussels Convention which would have the result that certain claims under a contract concluded by a consumer fall within the jurisdiction rules of Articles 13 to 15 of that Convention, whereas other actions that are linked so closely to that contract as to be indissociable are subject to other rules cannot be accepted.

57. The Court has in this regard recently recalled the need to avoid, so far as possible, a situation in which several courts have jurisdiction in respect of one and the same contract (see, by way of analogy, with regard to Article 5(1) of the Brussels Convention, Case C-256/00 *Besix* [2002] ECR I-0000, paragraph 27).

58. That need is all the more compelling in the case of a contract such as that in issue in the main proceedings. In view of the fact that a multiplicity of courts having jurisdiction risks placing at a particular disadvantage a party deemed to be weak, such as a consumer, it is in the interest of the proper administration of justice that the latter should be able to bring before one and the same court - *in casu* that of his place of domicile - all of the difficulties that are likely to arise from a contract which the consumer has been induced to conclude by reason of the professional's use of forms of wording liable to mislead the other contracting party.

59. An action such as that which Mr Gabriel proposes to bring before the competent national court therefore falls within the scope of Article 13, first paragraph, point 3, of the Brussels Convention, and it is for that reason unnecessary to examine whether it is covered by Article 5(1) thereof.

60. In the light of all the foregoing considerations, the answer to the question submitted must be that the jurisdiction rules set out in the Brussels Convention are to be construed as meaning that judicial proceedings by which a consumer seeks an order, in the Contracting State in which he is domiciled and pursuant to that State's legislation, requiring a mail-order company established in another Contracting State to pay him a financial benefit in circumstances where that company had sent to that

consumer in person a letter likely to create the impression that a prize would be awarded to him on condition that he ordered goods to a specified amount, and where that consumer actually placed such an order in the State of his domicile without, however, obtaining payment of that financial benefit, are contractual in nature in the sense contemplated in Article 13, first paragraph, point 3, of the Brussels Convention.

On those grounds,

THE COURT (Sixth Chamber),

in answer to the question referred to it by the Oberster Gerichtshof by order of 15 February 2000, hereby rules:

> **The jurisdiction rules set out in the Convention of 27 September 1968 on Jurisdiction and the Enforcement of Judgments in Civil and Commercial Matters, as amended by the Convention of 9 October 1978 on the Accession of the Kingdom of Denmark, Ireland and the United Kingdom of Great Britain and Northern Ireland, by the Convention of 25 October 1982 on the Accession of the Hellenic Republic, by the Convention of 26 May 1989 on the Accession of the Kingdom of Spain and the Portuguese Republic, and by the Convention of 29 November 1996 on the Accession of the Republic of Austria, the Republic of Finland and the Kingdom of Sweden, are to be construed as meaning that judicial proceedings by which a consumer seeks an order, in the Contracting State in which he is domiciled and pursuant to that State's legislation, requiring a mail-order company established in another Contracting State to pay him a financial benefit in circumstances where that company had sent to that consumer in person a letter likely to create the impression that a prize would be awarded to him on condition that he ordered goods to a specified amount, and where that consumer actually placed such an order in the State of his domicile without, however, obtaining payment of that financial benefit, are contractual in nature in the sense contemplated in Article 13, first paragraph, point 3, of that Convention.**

Case C-334/00 - 17 September 2002

Fonderie Officine Meccaniche Tacconi SpA
v
Heinrich Wagner Sinto Maschinenfabrik GmbH (HWS)

Article 5(1) and (3) - Special jurisdiction - Pre-contractual liability

JUDGMENT OF THE COURT

Rodríguez Iglesias, President, Colneric and von Bahr (Presidents of Chambers), Gulmann, Edward, La Pergola, Puissochet, Wathelet, Schintgen, Cunha Rodrigues (Rapporteur) and Timmermans, Judges

1. By order of 9 June 2000, received at the Court on 11 September 2000, the Corte suprema di cassazione (Court of Cassation) referred to the Court for a preliminary ruling under the Protocol of 3 June 1971 on the interpretation by the Court of Justice of the Convention of 27 September 1968 on Jurisdiction and the Enforcement ofJudgments in Civil and Commercial Matters (OJ 1978 L 304, p. 36) three questions on the interpretation of Article 5(1) and (3) of that convention, as amended by the Convention of 9 October 1978 on the Accession of the Kingdom of Denmark, Ireland and the United Kingdom of Great Britain and Northern Ireland (OJ 1978 L 304, p. 1 and - amended version - p. 77), by the Convention of 25 October 1982 on the Accession of the Hellenic Republic (OJ 1982 L 388, p. 1) and by the Convention of 26 May 1989 on the Accession of the Kingdom of Spain and the Portuguese Republic (OJ 1989 L 285, p. 1) (hereinafter 'the Brussels Convention').

2. Those questions were raised in proceedings between Fonderie Officine Meccaniche Tacconi SpA ('Tacconi'), a company incorporated under Italian law, established in Perugia (Italy), and Heinrich Wagner Sinto Maschinenfabrik GmbH ('HWS'), a company incorporated under German law, established in the Federal Republic of Germany, concerning

compensation claimed from HWS by Tacconi to make good the damage allegedly caused to Tacconi by HWS's breach of its duty to act honestly and in good faith on the occasion of negotiations with a view to the formation of a contract.

Legal background

The Brussels Convention

3. The first paragraph of Article 2 of the Brussels Convention provides:

'Subject to the provisions of this Convention, persons domiciled in a Contracting State shall, whatever their nationality, be sued in the courts of that State.'

4. Article 5(1) and (3) of the Brussels Convention provides:

'A person domiciled in a Contracting State may, in another Contracting State, be sued:

1. in matters relating to a contract, in the courts for the place of performance of the obligation in question; ...

...

3. in matters relating to tort, delict or quasi-delict, in the courts for the place where the harmful event occurred'.

National law

5. Article 1337 of the Italian Codice Civile (Civil Code) provides that, in the context of the negotiation and formation of a contract, the parties must act in good faith.

The main proceedings and the questions referred for a preliminary ruling

6. On 23 January 1996 Tacconi brought an action against HWS in the Tribunale di Perugia (District Court, Perugia) for a declaration that a contract between HWS and a leasing company B.N. Commercio e Finanza SpA ('BN') for the sale of a moulding plant, in respect of which BN and Tacconi had already, with the agreement of HWS, concluded a leasing contract, had not been concluded because of HWS's unjustified refusal to carry out the sale, and hence its breach of its duty to act honestly and in good faith. HWS thereby infringed the legitimate expectations of Tacconi, which had relied on the contract of sale being concluded. Tacconi therefore asked the court to order HWS to make

good all the damage allegedly caused, which was calculated at ITL 3 000 000 000.

7. In its defence, HWS pleaded that the Italian court lacked jurisdiction because of the existence of an arbitration clause and, in the alternative, because Article 5(1) of the Brussels Convention was applicable. On the substance, it contended that Tacconi's claim should be dismissed and, 'strictly in the alternative and as a counterclaim', that Tacconi should be ordered to pay it DEM 450 248.36.

8. By application served on 16 March 1999, Tacconi applied, pursuant to Article 41 of the Italian Codice di Procedura Civile (Code of Civil Procedure) concerning preliminary decisions on jurisdiction, to the Corte suprema di cassazione for a declaration that the Italian courts had jurisdiction over the main proceedings. Tacconi claimed that no agreement had been reached between it and HWS because its proposals had all been met by counter-proposals. It therefore relied on the pre-contractual liability of HWS on the basis of Article 1337 of the Italian Civil Code and submitted that under Article 5(3) of the Brussels Convention the 'place where the harmful event occurred' must also be understood as the place where the person claiming to have been harmed has sustained loss. The loss at issue in the main proceedings was incurred in Perugia, where Tacconi has its office.

9. In its order for reference, the national court considered that the criterion for special jurisdiction in Article 5(1) of the Brussels Convention does not appear to apply to pre-contractual liability, which does not result from the non-performance of a contractual obligation. No such obligation existed in the case at issue in the main proceedings, since no contract was concluded.

10. Since it considered that an interpretation of the Brussels Convention was thus needed in order to decide the issue of jurisdiction, the Corte suprema di cassazione decided to stay proceedings and refer the following questions to the Court for a preliminary ruling:

'1. Does an action against a defendant seeking to establish pre-contractual liability fall within the scope of matters relating to tort, delict or quasi-delict (Article 5(3) of the Brussels Convention)?

2. If not, does it fall within the scope of matters relating to a contract (Article 5(1) of the Brussels Convention), and if it does, what is the obligation in question?

3. If not, is the general criterion of the domicile of the defendant the only criterion applicable?'

Question 1

11. By its first question the national court asks whether an action founded on the pre-contractual liability of the defendant is a matter relating to tort, delict or quasi-delict within the meaning of Article 5(3) of the Brussels Convention.

Observations submitted to the Court

12. Tacconi and the Commission submit, citing the case-law of the Court (Case 189/87 *Kalfelis* [1988] ECR 5565, Case C-261/90 *Reichert and Kockler* [1992] ECR I-2149, and Case C-26/91 *Handte* [1992] ECR I-3967), that since pre-contractual liability does not derive from obligations freely assumed by one party towards another, it is a matter relating to tort, delict or quasi-delict.

13. According to Tacconi, it is quite plain that at the pre-contractual stage, since the contract has not yet been concluded, there is no contractual link which could bind the parties to each other.

14. The Commission submits that, on the basis of the Court's case-law, it is possible to state a general principle that all claims referred to by the Brussels Convention seeking to establish the liability of a defendant give rise, in any event, to the application of one of the two criteria of special jurisdiction in Article 5(1) and (3) of the convention.

15. The Commission concludes that disputes concerning pre-contractual liability fall within the scope of Article 5(3) of the Brussels Convention, since, first, an action founded on the defendant's pre-contractual liability is by definition a claim seeking to establish liability on the part of the defendant and, second, that liability is not based on obligations freely assumed by the defendant towards the claimant, but on duties as to conduct imposed, more or less specifically, by a source external to the parties involved in the pre-contractual relationship.

16. HWS submits, on the other hand, that pre-contractual liability is of a different nature from liability in tort, delict or quasi-delict. The latter applies to any person who breaches the general rule against causing harm to others and infringes 'absolute' rights.

17. Pre-contractual liability, however, may be imputed only to a person who has a special relationship with the person who has suffered harm, namely that resulting from the negotiation of a contract. Consequently, by contrast with the principles applicable to matters relating to tort, delict or quasi-delict, pre-contractual liability cannot be assessed except by reference to the content of the negotiations.

18. Moreover, submitting that Article 5(1) of the Brussels Convention cannot be applied either in this case, since Tacconi's claim rests on the hypothesis that no contract was concluded, HWS argues that pre-contractual liability is neither liability in tort, delict or quasi-delict nor liability in contract, and that the German courts therefore have jurisdiction to hear the case in accordance with the general provision in Article 2 of the Convention.

Findings of the Court

19. It should be observed at the outset that the Court has consistently held (see Case 34/82 *Martin Peters Bauunternehmung* [1983] ECR 987, paragraphs 9 and 10, *Reichert and Kockler*, paragraph 15, and *Handte*, paragraph 10) that the expressions 'matters relating to a contract' and 'matters relating to tort, delict or quasi-delict' in Article 5(1) and (3) of the Brussels Convention are to be interpreted independently, having regard primarily to the objectives and general scheme of the Convention. Those expressions cannot therefore be taken as simple references to the national law of one or the other of the Contracting States concerned.

20. Only such an interpretation is capable of ensuring the uniform application of the Brussels Convention, which is intended in particular to lay down common rules on jurisdiction for the courts of the Contracting States and to strengthen the legal protection of persons established in the Community by enabling the claimant to identify easily the court in which he may sue and the defendant reasonably to foresee in which court he may be sued (see Case C-295/95 *Farrell* [1997] ECR I-1683, paragraph 13, and Case C-256/00 *Besix* [2002] ECR I-1737, paragraphs 25 and 26).

21. As the Court has held, the concept of 'matters relating to tort, delict or quasi-delict' within the meaning of Article 5(3) of the Brussels Convention covers all actions which seek to establish the liability of a defendant and which are not related to a 'contract' within the meaning of Article 5(1) of the Convention (*Kalfelis*, paragraph 18, *Reichert and*

Kockler, paragraph 16, and Case C-51/97 *Réunion Européenne and Others* [1998] ECR I-6511, paragraph 22).

22. Moreover, while Article 5(1) of the Brussels Convention does not require a contract to have been concluded, it is nevertheless essential, for that provision to apply, to identify an obligation, since the jurisdiction of the national court is determined, in matters relating to a contract, by the place of performance of the obligation in question.

23. Furthermore, it should be noted that, according to the Court's case-law, the expression 'matters relating to contract' within the meaning of Article 5(1) of the Brussels Convention is not to be understood as covering a situation in which there is no obligation freely assumed by one party towards another (*Handte*, paragraph 15, and *Réunion Européenne and Others*, paragraph 17).

24. It does not appear from the documents in the case that there was any obligation freely assumed by HWS towards Tacconi.

25. In view of the circumstances of the main proceedings, the obligation to make good the damage allegedly caused by the unjustified breaking off of negotiations could derive only from breach of rules of law, in particular the rule which requires the parties to act in good faith in negotiations with a view to the formation of a contract.

26. In those circumstances, it is clear that any liability which may follow from the failure to conclude the contract referred to in the main proceedings cannot be contractual.

27. In the light of all the foregoing, the answer to the first question must be that, in circumstances such as those of the main proceedings, characterised by the absence of obligations freely assumed by one party towards another on the occasion of negotiations with a view to the formation of a contract and by a possible breach of rules of law, in particular the rule which requires the parties to act in good faith in such negotiations, an action founded on the pre-contractual liability of the defendant is a matter relating to tort, delict or quasi-delict within the meaning of Article 5(3) of the Brussels Convention.

Questions 2 and 3

28. As the first question has been answered in the affirmative, there is no need to answer the other questions put by the national court.

On those grounds,

THE COURT,

in answer to the questions referred to it by the Corte suprema di cassazione by order of 9 June 2000, hereby rules:

In circumstances such as those of the main proceedings, characterised by the absence of obligations freely assumed by one party towards another on the occasion of negotiations with a view to the formation of a contract and by a possible breach of rules of law, in particular the rule which requires the parties to act in good faith in such negotiations, an action founded on the pre-contractual liability of the defendant is a matter relating to tort, delict or quasi-delict within the meaning of Article 5(3) of the Convention of 27 September 1968 on Jurisdiction and the Enforcement of Judgments in Civil and Commercial Matters, as amended by the Convention of 9 October 1978 on the Accession of the Kingdom of Denmark, Ireland and the United Kingdom of Great Britain and Northern Ireland, by the Convention of 25 October 1982 on the Accession of the Hellenic Republic and by the Convention of 26 May 1989 on the Accession of the Kingdom of Spain and the Portuguese Republic.

Case C-167/00 - 1 October 2002

Verein für Konsumenteninformation
v
Karl Heinz Henkel

Article 5(3) - Jurisdiction in matters relating to tort, delict or quasi-delict - Preventive action by associations - Consumer protection organisation seeking an injunction to prevent a trader from using unfair terms in consumer contracts

JUDGMENT OF THE COURT (Sixth Chamber)

Macken, President of the Chamber, Gulmann, Puissochet, Schintgen (Rapporteur) and Cunha Rodrigues, Judges

1. By order of 13 April 2000, received at the Court on 8 May 2000, the Oberster Gerichtshof (Supreme Court, Austria) referred to the Court for a preliminary ruling, under the Protocol of 3 June 1971 on the interpretation by the Court of Justice of the Convention of 27 September 1968 on Jurisdiction and the Enforcement of Judgments in Civil and Commercial Matters, a question on the interpretation of Article 5(3) of that Convention (OJ 1978 L 304, p. 36), as amended by the Convention of 9 October 1978 on the Accession of the Kingdom of Denmark, Ireland and the United Kingdom of Great Britain and Northern Ireland (OJ 1978 L 304, p. 1, and - amended version - p. 77), by the Convention of 25 October 1982 on the Accession of the Hellenic Republic (OJ 1982 L 388, p. 1), by the Convention of 26 May 1989 on the Accession of the Kingdom of Spain and the Portuguese Republic (OJ 1989 L 285, p. 1) and by the Convention of 29 November 1996 on the Accession of the Republic of Austria, the Republic of Finland and the Kingdom of Sweden (OJ 1997 C 15, p. 1) ('the Brussels Convention').

2. That question was raised in proceedings between the Verein für Konsumenteninformation ('the VKI'), an association constituted under Austrian law, established in Austria, and Mr Henkel, a German national domiciled in Germany, concerning Mr Henkel's use in contracts concluded with Austrian consumers of terms which the VKI considered to be unfair.

Legal background

The Brussels Convention

3. The first paragraph of Article 1 of the Brussels Convention, which comprises Title I, entitled 'Scope', states:

'This convention shall apply in civil and commercial matters whatever the nature of the court or tribunal. It shall not extend, in particular, to revenue, customs or administrative matters.'

4. The rules on jurisdiction laid down by the Brussels Convention are set out in Title II thereof, which consists of Articles 2 to 24.

5. The first paragraph of Article 2, which forms part of Section 1, entitled 'General provisions', of Title II of the Brussels Convention, sets out the basic rule in the following terms:

'Subject to the provisions of this convention, persons domiciled in a Contracting State shall, whatever their nationality, be sued in the courts of that State.'

6. The first paragraph of Article 3 of the Brussels Convention, which appears in the same section, provides as follows:

'Persons domiciled in a Contracting State may be sued in the courts of another Contracting State only by virtue of the rules set out in Sections 2 to 6 of this title.'

7. Articles 5 to 18 of the Brussels Convention, which make up Sections 2 to 6 of Title II thereof, lay down rules governing special, mandatory or exclusive jurisdiction.

8. Section 2, entitled 'Special jurisdiction, of Title II of the Brussels Convention:

'A person domiciled in a Contracting State may, in another Contracting State, be sued:

1. in matters relating to a contract, in the courts for the place of performance of the obligation in question ...

...

3. in matters relating to tort, delict or quasi-delict, in the courts of the place where the harmful event occurred;

....'

Directive 93/13/EEC

9. Article 7(1) and (2) of Council Directive 93/13/EEC of 5 April 1993 on unfair terms in consumer contracts (OJ 1993 L 95, p. 29) provides:

'1. Member States shall ensure that, in the interests of consumers and of competitors, adequate and effective means exist to prevent the continued use of unfair terms in contracts concluded with consumers by sellers or suppliers.

2. The means referred to in paragraph 1 shall include provisions whereby persons or organisations, having a legitimate interest under national law in protecting consumers, may take action according to the national law concerned before the courts or before competent administrative bodies for a decision as to whether contractual terms drawn up for general use are unfair, so that they can apply appropriate and effective means to prevent the continued use of such terms.'

The relevant provisions of national law

10. In Austria, the Konsumentenschutzgesetz (Consumer Protection Law) of 8 March 1979 (BGBl. 1979/140; 'the KSchG) came into force on 1 October 1979.

11. The KSchG has been amended on several occasions, *inter alia* by a law transposing Directive 93/13 (BGBl. 1997/6).

12. Paragraph 28 of the KSchG, as amended, provides, with effect from 1 January 1997:

'(1) An injunction may be sought against anyone who in commercial dealings lays down, in general terms and conditions which he uses as a basis for contracts concluded by him or in forms used for contracts in that connection, conditions which are contrary to a statutory prohibition or are unconscionable, and against anyone who recommends such conditions for commercial dealings. This prohibition shall also include the prohibition on relying on such a condition in so far as it has been agreed to in an impermissible manner.

(2) There ceases to be any danger of the use and recommendation of such conditions where a trader gives, within a reasonable period, a declaration of discontinuance secured by an appropriate contractual penalty (Paragraph 1336 of the Allgemeines Bürgerliches Gesetzbuch) following a warning by a body entitled to bring an action under Paragraph 29.'

13. The VKI is one of the bodies referred to in Paragraph 29 of the KSchG which are entitled to bring such an action.

The main proceedings and the question referred for a preliminary ruling

14. It is clear from the documents relating to the case in the main proceedings that the VKI is a non-profit-making organisation whose object is the protection of consumers and their interests.

15. Mr Henkel is a trader, domiciled in Munich (Germany), who organises sales-promotion trips, *inter alia* in Austria.

16. In the context of his contractual dealings with consumers domiciled in Vienna (Austria), Mr Henkel used general terms and conditions that the VKI considers to be contrary to certain provisions of Austrian legislation.

17. As an association, the VKI brought an action pursuant to Paragraph 28 of the KSchG before the Handelsgericht Wien (Commercial Court, Vienna), seeking an injunction against Mr Henkel to prevent him from using the contested terms in contracts concluded with Austrian clients.

18. Mr Henkel claimed that the Austrian courts had no jurisdiction. In his submission, the action brought by the VKI cannot be regarded as relating to tort, delict or quasi-delict within the meaning of Article 5(3) of the Brussels Convention on the ground that there has been neither harmful behaviour nor damage suffered within the territorial jurisdiction of the court seized.

19. The Handelsgericht Wien found that the VKI was not pleading any damage arising out of a tort or delict and hence declared that it had no jurisdiction.

20. That decision was overturned on appeal by the Oberlandesgericht Wien (Higher Regional Court, Vienna) which considered that Article 5(3) of the Brussels Convention also covers preventive actions brought by an association such as the VKI without requiring it to have personally sustained any damage.

21. An appeal on a point of law was brought before the Oberster Gerichtshof which is uncertain whether the action at issue in the main proceedings falls within the scope of Article 5(3) of the Brussels Convention or whether it is a matter relating to a contract within the meaning of Article 5(1) of that convention.

22. According to that court it is not obvious that that action is a matter relating to tort or delict. The VKI does not plead any damage to its property. While it is true that its right to bring an action stems not from a contract, but from statute, and serves to avert future damage to consumers, such damage is none the less contractual in origin. The application of Article 5(1) of the Brussels Convention is therefore conceivable. However, it is also possible to consider that the unlawful act consists of the undermining of legal stability by a trader's use of unfair terms.

23. Moreover, the question arises whether a preventive action, which is by its very nature brought before any damage occurs, is capable of coming within the scope of Article 5(3) of the Brussels Convention, given that that provision, which refers to the place where the harmful event occurred, appears to presuppose the existence of damage.

24. The Oberster Gerichtshof took the view that, in those circumstances, the outcome of the case before it required an interpretation of the Brussels Convention and it therefore decided to stay proceedings and to refer the following question to the Court for a preliminary ruling:

'Does the right to obtain an injunction to prohibit the use of unlawful or unconscionable general terms and conditions provided for in Paragraph 28 of the [KSchG], which is asserted by a consumer protection organisation pursuant to Paragraph 29 of the KSchG and in accordance with Article 7(2) of ... Directive 93/13/EEC ..., constitute a claim arising out of matters relating to tort, delict or quasi-delict which may be asserted in courts with the special jurisdiction provided for in Article 5(3) of the Brussels Convention ... ?'

The national court's question

25. The first point to be noted is that the United Kingdom Government

submits that an action such as that brought by the VKI does not fall within the scope of the Brussels Convention. Pursuant to the first paragraph of Article 1 thereof, that convention applies only 'in civil and commercial matters', whereas a consumer protection organisation such as the VKI must be regarded as a public authority and its right to obtain an injunction to prevent the use of unfair terms in contracts, which is exercised in the main proceedings, constitutes a public law power. An organisation of that kind takes on the task, in the public interest, of ensuring the protection of the entire class of consumers, and its right to bring proceedings to obtain an injunction preventing unlawful behaviour by traders stems from statute, independent of any private law relationship arising out of a contract between a professional and a private individual.

26. However, it is settled case-law that actions between a public authority and a person governed by private law fall outside the scope of the Brussels Convention only in so far as that authority is acting in the exercise of public powers (see, to that effect, Case 29/76 *LTU* v *Eurocontrol* [1976] ECR 1541, paragraph 4; Case 814/79 *Rüffer* [1980] ECR 3807, paragraph 8, and Case C-172/91 *Sonntag* [1993] ECR I-1963, paragraph 20).

27. That is the case in a dispute which concerns the recovery of charges payable by a person governed by private law to a national or international body governed by pubic law for the use of equipment and services provided by that body, in particular where such use is obligatory and exclusive (see *LTU*, cited above, paragraph 4).

28. Similarly, the Court has held that the concept of 'civil and commercial matters' within the meaning of the first paragraph of Article 1 of the Brussels Convention does not include actions brought by the State responsible for administering public waterways against a person having liability in law in order to recover the costs incurred in the removal of a wreck carried out by or at the instigation of that administering agent in the exercise of its public authority (*Rüffer*, cited above, paragraphs 9 and 16).

29. Although it thus follows from the case-law of the Court that certain types of dispute must be regarded as excluded from the scope of the Brussels Convention, by reason either of the legal relationships between the parties to the action or of the subject-matter of the action (see *LTU*, paragraph 4), the case-law arising from *LTU* and *Rüffer* cannot be applied to an action such as that at issue in the main proceedings.

30. Not only is a consumer protection organisation such as the VKI a private body, but in addition, as the German Government correctly observed, the subject-matter of the main proceedings is not an exercise of public powers, since those proceedings do not in any way concern the exercise of powers derogating from the rules of law applicable to relations between private individuals. On the contrary, the action pending before the national court concerns the prohibition on traders' using unfair terms in their contracts with consumers and thus seeks to make relationships governed by private law subject to review by the courts. Hence, an action of that kind is a civil matter within the meaning of the first paragraph of Article 1 of the Brussels Convention.

31. In those circumstances, the objection raised by the United Kingdom Government cannot be accepted.

32. As to the question referred by the national court, it should be noted at the outset that Articles 13 to 15, which comprise Section 4, entitled 'Jurisdiction over consumer contracts', of Title II of the Brussels Convention, are not applicable in the main proceedings.

33. As the Court held in Case C-89/91 *Shearson Lehman Hutton* [1993] ECR I-139, a legal person which acts as assignee of the rights of a private final consumer, without itself being party to a contract between a professional and a private individual, cannot be regarded as a consumer within the meaning of the Brussels Convention and therefore cannot invoke Articles 13 to 15 of that convention. That interpretation must also apply in respect of a consumer protection organisation such as the VKI which has brought an action as an association on behalf of consumers.

34. It follows that, in order to answer the question referred by the national court, it need only be determined whether a preventive action brought by a consumer protection organisation for the purpose of preventing a trader from using terms considered to be unfair in contracts with private individuals is a matter relating to a contract within the meaning of Article 5(1) of the Brussels Convention, or in fact a matter relating to tort, delict or quasi-delict within the meaning of Article 5(3) of that convention.

35. In that regard, the Court has repeatedly held that the concepts of 'matters relating to a contract' and 'matters relating to tort, delict or quasi-delict' in paragraphs 1 and 3 respectively of Article 5 of the Brussels Convention are to be interpreted independently, having regard

primarily to the objectives and general scheme of that convention, in order to ensure that it is both given full effect and applied uniformly in all the Contracting States (see, in particular, Case 34/82 *Peters* [1983] ECR 987, paragraphs 9 and 10; Case 189/87 *Kalfelis* [1988] ECR 5565, paragraphs 15 and 16, and Case C-261/90 *Reichert and Kockler* [1992] ECR I-2149, paragraph 15).

36. It is also settled case-law that the concept of matters relating to tort, delict or quasi-delict within the meaning of Article 5(3) of the Brussels Convention covers all actions which seek to establish the liability of a defendant and are not matters relating to a contract within the meaning of Article 5(1) of that convention (see, in particular, *Kalfelis*, cited above, paragraph 17; *Reichert and Kockler*, cited above, paragraph 16; Case C-51/97 *Réunion Européenne and Others* [1998] ECR I-6511, paragraph 22, and Case C-96/00 *Gabriel* [2002] ECR I-0000, paragraph 33).

37. It is therefore necessary in the first instance to examine whether an action such as that at issue in the main proceedings is contractual in nature.

38. In a situation such as that in the main proceedings, the consumer protection organisation and the trader are in no way linked by any contractual relationship.

39. Admittedly, it is likely that the trader has already entered into contracts with a number of consumers. However, whether the court action is subsequent to a contract already concluded between the trader and a consumer or that action is purely preventive in nature and its sole aim is to prevent the occurrence of future damage, the consumer protection organisation which brought that action is never itself a party to the contract. The legal basis for its action is a right conferred by statute for the purpose of preventing the use of terms which the legislature considers to be unlawful in dealings between a professional and a private final consumer.

40. In those circumstances, an action such as that brought in the main proceedings cannot be regarded as a matter relating to a contract within the meaning of Article 5(1) of the Brussels Convention.

41. By contrast, such an action meets all the criteria established by the Court in the case-law referred to in paragraph 36 of this judgment inasmuch as, first, it does not concern matters relating to a contract within the meaning of Article 5(1) of the Brussels Convention and, second, it seeks

to establish the liability of the defendant in tort, delict or quasi-delict, in the present case in respect of the trader's non-contractual obligation to refrain in his dealings with consumers from certain behaviour deemed unacceptable by the legislature.

42. The concept of 'harmful event' within the meaning of Article 5(3) of the Brussels Convention is broad in scope (Case 21/76 *Bier* ('*Mines de Potasse d'Alsace*) [1976] ECR 1735, paragraph 18) so that, with regard to consumer protection, it covers not only situations where an individual has personally sustained damage but also, in particular, the undermining of legal stability by the use of unfair terms which it is the task of associations such as the VKI to prevent.

43. Furthermore, that is the only interpretation consistent with the purpose of Article 7 of Directive 93/13. Accordingly, the efficacy of the actions under that provision to prevent the continued use of unlawful terms would be considerably diminished if those actions could be brought only in the State where the trader is domiciled.

44. Mr Henkel and the French Government have, however, submitted that Article 5(3) of the Brussels Convention refers to the place where the harmful event occurred and therefore presupposes, according to its actual terms, the existence of damage. They argue that the same conclusion is dictated by the Court's interpretation of that provision, according to which the expression 'place where the harmful event occurred' must be understood as being intended to cover both the place where the damage occurred and the place of the event giving rise to that damage, so that the defendant may be sued, at the option of the plaintiff, in the courts for either of those places (see, in particular, *Mines de Potasse d'Alsace*, cited above, paragraphs 24 and 25; Case C-220/88 *Dumez France and Tracoba* [1990] ECR I-49, paragraph 10; Case C-68/93 *Shevill and Others* [1995] ECR I-415, paragraph 20, and Case C-364/93 *Marinari* [1995] ECR I-2719, paragraph 11). In their submission, it follows that Article 5(3) of the Brussels Convention cannot be applied to purely preventive actions which are brought before any actual damage has occurred and are intended to prevent the occurrence of a future harmful event.

45. That objection is not however well founded.

46. The rule of special jurisdiction laid down in Article 5(3) of the Brussels Convention is based on the existence of a particularly close con-

necting factor between a dispute and the courts for the place where the harmful event occurred, which justifies the attribution of jurisdiction to those courts for reasons relating to the sound administration of justice and the efficacious conduct of proceedings (see to that effect, *inter alia*, *Mines de Potasse d'Alsace*, paragraphs 11 and 17; *Dumez France and Tracoba*, paragraph 17; *Shevill and Others*, paragraph 19, and *Marinari*, paragraph 10). The courts for the place where the harmful event occurred are usually the most appropriate for deciding the case, in particular on the grounds of proximity and ease of taking evidence. Those considerations are equally relevantwhether the dispute concerns compensation for damage which has already occurred or relates to an action seeking to prevent the occurrence of damage.

47. That interpretation is moreover supported by the Report by Professor Schlosser on the Convention on the Accession of the Kingdom of Denmark, Ireland and the United Kingdom of Great Britain and Northern Ireland to the Brussels Convention (OJ 1979 C 59, pp. 71, 111), which states that Article 5(3) of the Brussels Convention also covers actions whose aim is to prevent the imminent commission of a tort (or delict).

48. It is therefore not possible to accept an interpretation of Article 5(3) of the Brussels Convention according to which application of that provision is conditional on the actual occurrence of damage. Furthermore, it would be inconsistent to require that an action to prevent behaviour considered to be unlawful, such as that brought in the main proceedings, whose principal aim is precisely to prevent damage, may be brought only after that damage has occurred.

49. Finally, Council Regulation (EC) No 44/2001 of 22 December 2000 on jurisdiction and the recognition and enforcement of judgments in civil and commercial matters (OJ 2001 L 12, p. 1), while not applicable *ratione temporis* to the main proceedings, is such as to confirm the interpretation that Article 5(3) of the Brussels Convention does not presuppose the existence of damage. That regulation clarified the wording of Article 5(3) of the Brussels Convention that the new version of that provision resulting from that regulation refers to 'the place where the harmful event occurred or may occur'. In the absence of any reason for interpreting the two provisions in question differently, consistency requires that Article 5(3) of the Brussels Convention be given a scope identical to that of the equivalent provision of Regulation No 44/2001. This is all the more necessary given that that regulation is intended to replace the

Brussels Convention in relations between Member States with the exception of the Kingdom of Denmark, with that convention continuing to apply between the Kingdom of Denmark and the Member States bound by that regulation.

50. In the light of all the foregoing considerations, the answer to the question referred by the national court must be that the rules on jurisdiction laid down in the Brussels Convention must be interpreted as meaning that a preventive action brought by a consumer protection organisation for the purpose of preventing a trader from using terms considered to be unfair in contracts with private individuals is a matter relating to tort, delict or quasi-delict within the meaning of Article 5(3) of that convention.

On those grounds,

THE COURT (Sixth Chamber),

in answer to the question referred to it by the Oberster Gerichtshof by order of 13 April 2000, hereby rules:

> **The rules on jurisdiction laid down in the Convention of 27 September 1968 on Jurisdiction and the Enforcement of Judgments in Civil and Commercial Matters of 27 September 1968, as amended by the Convention of 9 October 1978 on the Accession of the Kingdom of Denmark, Ireland and the United Kingdom of Great Britain and Northern Ireland, by the Convention of 25 October 1982 on the Accession of the Hellenic Republic, by the Convention of 26 May 1989 on the Accession of the Kingdom of Spain and the Portuguese Republic and by the Convention of 29 November 1996 on the Accession of the Republic of Austria, the Republic of Finland and the Kingdom of Sweden, must be interpreted as meaning that a preventive action brought by a consumer protection organisation for the purpose of preventing a trader from using terms considered to be unfair in contracts with private individuals is a matter relating to tort, delict or quasi-delict within the meaning of Article 5(3) of that convention.**

Case C-271/00 - 14 November 2002

Gemeente Steenbergen
v
Luc Baten

Scope of the Convention - Action under a right of recourse under national legislation providing for payment of allowances by way of social assistance - Concept of 'civil matters' - Concept of 'social security

JUDGMENT OF THE COURT (Fifth Chamber)

Timmermans, President of the Fourth Chamber, acting as President of the Fifth Chamber, Edward, La Pergola,Jann (Rapporteur) and von Bahr, Judges

1. By order of 27 June 2000, received at the Court on 5 July 2000, the Hof van Beroep te Antwerpen (Court of Appeal, Antwerp) referred to the Court for a preliminary ruling pursuant to the Protocol of 3 June 1971 on the interpretation by the Court of Justice of the Convention of 27 September 1968 on Jurisdiction and the Enforcement of Judgments in Civil and Commercial Matters two questions on the interpretation of Article 1 of the abovementioned Convention of 27 September 1968 (OJ 1978 L 304, p. 36), as amended by the Convention of 9 October 1978 on the Accession of the Kingdom of Denmark, Ireland and the United Kingdom of Great Britain and Northern Ireland (OJ 1978 L 304, p. 1 and - amended version - p. 77) and by the Convention of 25 October 1982 on the Accession of the Hellenic Republic (OJ 1982 L 388, p. 1) (hereinafter 'the Brussels Convention').

2. Those questions were raised in a legal action under a right of recourse brought by Gemeente Steenbergen, a Netherlands local authority, against Mr Baten, resident in Belgium, in order to recover sums of

money paid by that authority, by way of social assistance, to the divorced spouse and the child of Mr Baten.

Legal framework

The Brussels Convention

3. The scope of the Brussels Convention is defined in Article 1 thereof, which provides:

'This Convention shall apply in civil and commercial matters whatever the nature of the court or tribunal. It shall not extend, in particular, to revenue, customs or administrative matters.

The Convention shall not apply to:

...

3. social security;

...'

4. Under Article 26 of the Brussels Convention, a judgment given in a Contracting State is to be automatically recognised in the other Contracting States without any special procedure being required.

5. However, Article 27 of the Brussels Convention specifies exhaustively the cases in which recognition is to be refused. It is worded as follows:

'A judgment shall not be recognised:

...

3. if the judgment is irreconcilable with a judgment given in a dispute between the same parties in the State in which recognition is sought;

...'

6. Under Article 55 the Brussels Convention supersedes, for the States which are parties to it, certain conventions listed therein. These include 'the Convention between Belgium and the Netherlands on jurisdiction, bankruptcy and the validity and enforcement of judgments, arbitration awards and authentic instruments signed in Brussels on 28 March 1925' (hereinafter the Belgium–Netherlands Convention of 1925).

7. Under Article 56 of the Brussels Convention the conventions mentioned in Article 55 thereof are to continue to have effect in relation to matters to which the Brussels Convention does not apply.

Netherlands legislation

8. The Algemene Bijstandswet (Law on general assistance, *Staatsblad* 1995, No 1999, p. 1, hereinafter the 'ABW') establishes a system of social security in favour of persons residing in the Netherlands without resources.

9. General assistance (*algemene bijstand*) comprises a monthly contribution linked to the statutory minimum wage and intended to enable the recipient to meet the essential costs of subsistence. The assistance is granted by the municipality in which the person concerned is resident.

10. Article 93 of the ABW provides:

'The cost of assistance shall be recovered, up to the limit of the extent of the maintenance obligation under Book I of the Civil Code:

(a) from a person who, living apart from his family, does not, or does not fully, meet his maintenance obligation in respect of his spouse or infant child ...;

(b) from persons who do not, or do not fully, meet their maintenance obligations following a divorce ...;

(c) ...'

11. Article 94 of the ABW provides:

'An agreement under which spouses or former spouses stipulate that, after their divorce ..., they shall in no way be mutually bound by a maintenance obligation or that such obligation shall be limited to a specific amount, shall not preclude recovery ... from one of the parties and shall be without prejudice to determination of the amount to be recovered.'

12. Where the person against whom the municipality decides to seek recovery is not prepared to pay voluntarily, the municipality may bring an action under a right of recourse, in accordance with Article 102 et seq. of the ABW. Such action is governed by the rules of civil procedure.

The dispute in the main proceedings and the questions referred for a preliminary ruling

13. The marriage between Mr Baten and Mrs Kil was dissolved by a divorce decree granted by consent on 14 May 1987 by a Belgian court. In the agreement prior to the divorce entered into on 25 March 1986 before a notary established in Belgium, the spouses agreed that no maintenance

would be payable as between themselves and that Mr Baten would pay BEF 3 000 per month by way of contribution to the maintenance of the infant child of the marriage.

14. Mrs Kil and her child settled in the municipality of Steenbergen (Netherlands), which granted them an allowance by way of social assistance under the ABW.

15. Subsequently, the municipality of Steenbergen sought recovery from Mr Baten under Article 93 *et seq*. of the ABW of the amounts paid. Since Mr Baten did not accede to that claim, the municipality of Steenbergen brought an action under a right of recourse against him under Article 102 of the ABW before the Arrondissementstrechtbank te Breda (District Court, Breda) (Netherlands).

16. By order of 22 July 1996 the Arrondissementsrechtbank te Breda ordered Mr Baten to pay to the municipality of Steenbergen the amounts granted to Mrs Kil and her child by way of social assistance.

17. By order of 11 February 1998 the President of the Rechtbank van eerste aanleg te Turnhout (Court of First Instance, Turnhout) (Belgium) declared the order of 22 July 1996 enforceable.

18. Mr Baten appealed against that order. By judgments of 17 March and 23 June 1999 the Rechtbank van eerste aanleg te Turnhout declared that appeal well founded and held that enforcement of the order of 22 July 1996 of the Arrondissementsrechtbank te Breda was not possible 'owing to the incompatibility of that decision with the divorce decree by consent of 14 May 1987 which by implication includes and confirms the instrument notarised on 25 March 1986'.

19. The municipality of Steenbergen appealed against those two judgments to the Hof van Beroep te Antwerpen. It claimed that, since the dispute concerns a matter of social security it comes not within the scope of the Brussels Convention but within that of the Belgium–Netherlands Convention of 1925.

20. Under those circumstances the Hof van Beroep te Antwerpen decided to stay proceedings and refer the two following questions to the Court for a preliminary ruling:

'1. Is a legal action under a right of recourse under the Netherlands Algemene Bijstandswet (Law on General Assistance) brought by a municipality entitled to seek recovery against a person liable to pay maintenance, as referred to in Article 93 of the Algemene Bijstandswet, a civil matter within the meaning of the first paragraph of Article 1 of the Convention of 27 September 1968 on Jurisdiction and the Enforcement of Judgments in Civil and Commercial Matters, and does a judicial decision delivered in such an action come for that reason within the scope of that Convention?

2. Is a legal action under a right of recourse under the Netherlands Algemene Bijstandswet brought by a municipality entitled to seek recovery against a person liable to pay maintenance, as referred to in Article 93 of the Algemene Bijstandswet, a case relating to social security within the meaning of Article 1, second paragraph, point 3, of the Convention of 27 September 1968 on Jurisdiction and the Enforcement of Judgments in Civil and Commercial Matters, and does a judicial decision delivered in such an action for that reason fall outside the scope of that Convention?'

The first question

21. In this question the referring court is, essentially, seeking to ascertain whether the concept of 'civil matters' in the first paragraph of Article 1 of the Brussels Convention encompasses an action under a right of recourse under which a public body seeks recovery from a private person of sums paid by it by way of social assistance to the divorced spouse and the child of that person.

Observations submitted to the Court

22. In their observations to the Court the parties to the main proceedings, the Member States and the Commission are at one in acknowledging that the concept of 'civil matters' in Article 1 of the Brussels Convention must be defined autonomously. They are also at one in pointing out that disputes between the public authority and an individual may come within the scope of the Brussels Convention provided that the public authority has not acted in the exercise of its public powers.

23. However, the observations are at variance in regard to the application of those principles to the dispute in the main proceedings.

24. The municipality of Steenbergen and the United Kingdom Government maintain that a public authority which brings an action against an individual in order to recover sums paid by it by way of social assistance is acting in the exercise of its public powers.

25. The Commission, too, supported that view during the written procedure, on the basis of the fact that under the ABW the municipality granting social assistance has a broad discretion in determining both the persons entitled to and the amount of assistance, and in deciding whether or not to recover that amount. However, at the hearing it altered its view, basing itself on a different reading of the ABW. On that reading, the municipality is obliged to seek recovery once there is a person under a statutory obligation to pay maintenance, although the action under a right of recourse can be availed of only within the limits of the maintenance obligation not complied with by that person. The municipality is thus exercising a right of a civil-law nature.

26. The Austrian and Swedish Governments likewise contend that the action under a right of recourse in point here is linked to a civil-law right to maintenance, in the present case vested in Mrs Kil and her daughter *vis-à-vis* Mr Baten. The fact that that right was transferred to a public authority did not alter its character.

27. The Netherlands Government also contends that the action in point in the main proceedings is an action in a civil matter. However, it prefers to regard it as an action for reparation of the loss occasioned to the municipality concerned as a result of the fact that it had to pay an allowance by way of social assistance to a person without resources to whom maintenance was owed.

Findings of the Court

28. It is settled case-law that, since Article 1 of the Brussels Convention serves to indicate the area of application of the Convention, it is necessary, in order to ensure, as far as possible, that the rights and obligations which derive from it for the Contracting States and the persons to whom it applies are equal and uniform, that the terms of that provision should not be interpreted as a mere reference to the internal law of one or other of the States concerned. The concept referred to must therefore be regarded as an independent concept to be interpreted by reference, first, to the objectives and, secondly, to the general principles which stem from the national legal systems as a whole (Case 29/76 *LTU* [1976] ECR 1541, paragraph 3; Case 133/78 *Gourdain* [1979] ECR 733, paragraph 3; Case 814/79 *Rüffer* [1980] ECR 3807, paragraph 7; and Case C-172/91 *Sonntag* [1993] ECR I-1963, paragraph 18).

29. The Court has made it clear that that interpretation results in the

exclusion of certain judicial decisions from the scope of the Brussels Convention, owing either to the legal relationships between the parties to the action or to its subject-matter (*LTU*, cited above, paragraph 4).

30. Thus the Court has held that, although certain judgments in actions between a public authority and a person governed by private law may come within the scope of the Brussels Convention, it is otherwise where the public authority is acting in the exercise of its public powers (*LTU*, cited above, paragraph 4, and *Rüffer*, paragraph 8).

31. In order to determine whether that is so in a case such as that in point in the main proceedings, in which a public body seeks from a person governed by private law recovery of sums paid by it by way of social assistance to the former spouse and the child of that person, it is necessary to examine the basis and the detailed rules governing the bringing of that action.

32. In that regard, it appears from Article 93 of the ABW that the costs of social assistance are recoverable up to the limit of the maintenance obligation under Book I of the Netherlands Civil Code. Thus it is the rules of the civil law which determine the cases in which the public body may bring an action under a right of recourse, namely where there is a person under a statutory obligation to pay maintenance. It is on the basis of those same rules that the person against whom the public body may proceed, namely the person under a statutory obligation to pay maintenance, is identified, and that the limits to the amounts recoverable by that body are determined, those limits being coterminous with those of the statutory maintenance obligation itself.

33. As regards the detailed rules governing the bringing of an action under a right of recourse, Article 103 of the ABW states that that action must be brought before the civil courts and is that it governed by the rules of civil procedure.

34. Accordingly, as the Advocate General stated at paragraph 36 of his Opinion, the legal situation of the public body *vis-à-vis* the person liable for maintenance is comparable to that of an individual who, having paid on whatever ground another's debt, is subrogated to the rights of the original creditor, or is comparable to the situation of a person who, having suffered loss as a result of an act or omission imputable to a third party, seeks reparation from that party.

35. However, that finding calls for some qualification by reason of Article 94 of the ABW under which an agreement between spouses or former spouses for the purpose of precluding or limiting their maintenance obligations after their divorce does not preclude recovery from one of the parties and is without prejudice to determination of the amounts to be recovered.

36. To the extent to which that provision allows the public body, in a proper case, to disregard an agreement lawfully entered into between spouses or former spouses, producing binding effects between them and enforceable against third parties, it places the public body in a legal situation which derogates from the ordinary law. That is all the more so inasmuch as that provision allows the public body to disregard anagreement approved by a judicial decision and covered by the force of *res judicata* attaching to that decision. In those circumstances, the public body is no longer acting under rules of the civil law but under a prerogative of its own, specifically conferred on it by the legislature.

37. In light of the foregoing considerations, the reply to the first question must be that the first paragraph of Article 1 of the Brussels Convention must be interpreted as meaning that the concept of 'civil matters' encompasses an action under a right of recourse whereby a public body seeks from a person governed by private law recovery of sums paid by it by way of social assistance to the divorced spouse and the child of that person, provided that the basis and the detailed rules relating to the bringing of that action are governed by the rules of the ordinary law in regard to maintenance obligations. Where the action under a right of recourse is founded on provisions by which the legislature conferred on the public body a prerogative of its own, that action cannot be regarded as being brought in 'civil matters'.

Second question

38. In this question the referring court is, essentially, seeking to ascertain whether the concept of 'social security' at point 3 of the second paragraph of Article 1 of the Brussels Convention encompasses an action under a right of recourse by which a public body seeks from a person governed by private law recovery of sums paid by it by way of social assistance to the divorced spouse and the child of that person.

Observations submitted to the Court

39. The Netherlands, Austrian and United Kingdom Governments, and

the Commission, note that the Brussels Convention does not define the concept of 'social security' and refer in that regard to Article 4 of Council Regulation (EEC) No 1408/71 of 14 June 1971 on the application of social security schemes to employed persons, to self-employed persons and to members of their families moving within the Community, in the version as amended and updated by Council Regulation (EC) No 118/97 of 2 December 1996 (OJ 1997 L 28, p. 1, hereinafter 'Regulation No 1408/71').

40. Those governments maintain, none the less, as does the Commission, that the exclusion of social-security disputes from the scope of the Brussels Convention must be strictly construed. It concerns only disputes between the institutions and recipients of benefits and does not extend to actions brought by an institution against a third party.

Findings of the Court

41. As a preliminary point, it should be observed that a reply to this question is called for only if the public body is acting in accordance with the rules of the ordinary law and where the decision in the action under a right of recourse brought by it may be regarded as a decision in 'civil matters' under the first paragraph of Article 1 of the Brussels Convention.

42. Inasmuch as the concept of 'social security' serves to indicate the area of application of the Brussels Convention, it must, as the Court has stated at paragraph 28 above, be regarded as an independent concept, to be interpreted by reference to the objectives and scheme of the Brussels Convention.

43. In view of the link between the Brussels Convention and Community law (see Case C-398/92 *Mund & Fester* [1994] ECR I-467, paragraph 12, and Case C-7/98 *Krombach* [2000] ECR I-1935, paragraph 24), regard must be had to the substance of that concept in Community law.

44. By adopting Regulation No 1408/71 on the basis of Article 51 of the EEC Treaty (subsequently Article 51 of the EC Treaty, and now, after amendment, Article 42 EC), the Community legislature laid down rules coordinating national legislation on social security. As the Advocate General noted at paragraphs 46 and 47 of his Opinion, those rules establish a system under which as a matter of principle the exclusive legislative competence of a Member State is matched by the competence of the

administrative and judicial authorities of the same State. It follows that legal situations are effectively protected by the designation of a national system competent in its entirety and do not require recognition of judgments relating to that area.

45. It must therefore be held that the substance of the concept of 'social security' in the second paragraph of Article 1 of the Brussels Convention encompasses the matters covered by Regulation No 1408/71, as defined in Article 4 thereof and clarified in the Court's case-law.

46. However, irrespective of how, in the light of Article 4 of Regulation No 1408/71, benefits paid by way of social assistance by a public body to persons without resources are to be characterised, the action under a right of recourse brought by that body against a third party, a person governed by private law, as the subject of an obligation to pay maintenance to the persons assisted, is not concerned with the conditions under which the benefits in question are granted but with recovery of the sums paid in that regard.

47. It follows that, in any event, the subject-matter of the dispute does not concern the application of Regulation No 1408/71.

48. That interpretation is born out by both the Jenard Report on the Convention on Jurisdiction and the Enforcement of Judgments in Civil and Commercial Matters (OJ 1979 C 59, pp. 1, 12 and 13) and the Schlosser Report on the Convention on the accession of the Kingdom of Denmark, Ireland and the United Kingdom of Great Britain and Northern Ireland to the Brussels Convention (OJ 1979 C 59, p. 71, paragraph 60). According to those reports the exclusion of social security from thescope of the Brussels Convention concerns only litigation in that area, that is to say disputes arising out of the relationship between the administration and employers or employees. Those reports add that the Brussels Convention is applicable where the administration exercises a direct right of action against a third party liable for injury or is subrogated as regards that third party to the rights of a victim insured by it, because it is then acting under the rules of the ordinary law.

49. In the light of the foregoing considerations, the reply to the question submitted must be that point 3 of the second paragraph of Article 1 of the Brussels Convention must be interpreted as meaning that the concept of 'social security' does not encompass the action under a right of recourse by which a public body seeks from a person governed by private law recovery

in accordance with the rules of the ordinary law of sums paid by it by way of social assistance to the divorced spouse and the child of that person.

On those grounds,

THE COURT (Fifth Chamber),

in answer to the questions referred to it by the Hof van Beroep te Antwerpen by order of 27 June 2000, hereby rules:

1. The first paragraph of Article 1 of the Convention of 27 September 1968 on Jurisdiction and the Enforcement of Judgments in Civil and Commercial Matters, as amended by the Convention of 9 October 1978 on the Accession of the Kingdom of Denmark, Ireland and the United Kingdom of Great Britain and Northern Ireland and by the Convention of 25 October 1982 on the Accession of the Hellenic Republic, must be interpreted as meaning that the concept of 'civil matters' encompasses an action under a right of recourse whereby a public body seeks from a person governed by private law recovery of sums paid by it by way of social assistance to the divorced spouse and the child of that person, provided that the basis and the detailed rules relating to the bringing of that action are governed by the rules of the ordinary law in regard to maintenance obligations. Where the action under a right of recourse is founded on provisions by which the legislature conferred on the public body a prerogative of its own, that action cannot be regarded as being brought in 'civil matters'.

2. Point 3 of the second paragraph of Article 1 of the Brussels Convention must be interpreted as meaning that the concept of 'social security' does not encompass the action under a right of recourse by which a public body seeks from a person governed by private law recovery in accordance with the rules of the ordinary law of sums paid by it by way of social assistance to the divorced spouse and the child of that person.

JURISDICTION AND ENFORCEMENT OF JUDGMENTS IN CIVIL AND COMMERCIAL MATTERS

ECJ JUDGMENTS

SUPPLEMENT